THE ROOTS & RHYTHM
OF THE HEART

THE ROOTS & RHYTHM OF THE HEART

"It's easy to get caught up in the rhythm of life—traffic, work, politics, family—busy-ness filling our days and minds with noise. The din deafening, it can drown out the sounds that soothe—sounds of our source: our heartbeats. Whether through music, visual art, dance, or drama, when we focus on this beat and how it connects us— intertwining us despite our efforts to find categories to separate from and demean each other—our shared experiences on the planet cannot be ignored. Connections (within and without) are highlighted and can strengthen, providing space for healing. Dr. Demaine's insightful work draws attention to the sacred rhythm within each of us and its power to connect and heal. Resonant and rhythmic, it's a timely addition to the clinical bookshelf."

–Lillian Sylvester, Ph.D. LCPC,
Expressive Arts Therapist and Director of Teal Fire Counseling

"*The Roots & Rhythm of the Heart* offers a rich exploration for the journey of connecting to self, to lineage and ancestors, and to community. Through presentation of new and ancient traditions and philosophies, it provides a wide array of expressive arts techniques that are accessible for all readers. Dr. Demaine's poignant and moving personal narrative is woven throughout, and combines with her skillful, compassionate, and experienced voice to make this book a compelling read and valuable therapeutic guidance. An excellent resource for therapists, and for anyone interested in deepening their understanding of all that lies within the heart."

–Liz Owen, E-RYT500, C-IAYT
Author of The Yoga Effect: A Proven Program for Depression and Anxiety

"In *The Roots & Rhythm of the Heart*, Krystal Demaine leads the reader through meditation and Expressive Arts exercises, research, and prose toward healing. Because of her willingness to explore her own experience, we look at ourselves deeply. Read this book to make space in your life for healing the heart".

– Joan Hanley, MA, MFA
Exhibiting Artist, Teacher, and Author of Art and Yoga

"Music is integral to our self-awareness, our self-expression, and to healing the heart. At this time, when life can be challenging and chaotic, *The Roots and Rhythm of the Heart* will illuminate its readers.

–Dr. Rev. Gail Cantor, D.Min.
Director of Belonging and Spiritual Life, Endicott College

"There is no sound quite like the sweet melody of a beating heart pulsing with life. In *The Roots & Rhythm of the Heart*, Dr. Demaine encourages us to stop and listen. Woven through the pages, she poignantly shares the beautiful music discovered within her Dad's heart, as she journeyed with him through the end of life. Using music, yoga, journaling, and breath work, Dr. Demaine invites us to recognize and appreciate the beauty each heart has to offer."

– Maureen Burge, MS, CLS
Pediatric Palliative Care Child Life Specialist

THE ROOTS & RHYTHM OF THE HEART

Our Musical Connection to Identity, Spirit, and Lineage

Krystal L. Demaine, Ph.D.

THE ROOTS & RHYTHM OF THE HEART

Printed in the United States of America
First Printing, 2022

Book cover design by Danielle Currier
Author photo by Ezra Demaine

ISBN 979-8-9865128-1-5 *Hardcover*
ISBN 979-8-9865128-3-9 *Paperback*
ISBN 979-8-9865128-2-2 *eBook*

Published by Krystal L. Demaine
www.krystaldemaine.com

For my father,
Kenneth L. Demaine

Table of Contents

List of Creative Exercises   xiii
List of Illustrations   xiv
Acknowledgments   xv
Preface   xvi

1.   A CALL TO THE HEART   1
    The Heart is Calling   1
    Perpetual Music   4
    Entering into Heart Work   6

1.   THE HEARTS OCCUPATION   11
    Dancing with the Heart   11
    The Heart's Meaning   13
    The Yin-Yang Heart   15
    The Emotional Heart   17
    A Heart, a Home, the Nerve   18
    Tending to the Heart   20

2.   IT STARTS WITH THE PULSE   25
    The Eternal Rhythm of the Heart   25
    Recording the Sacred Heartbeat   27
    The Pulse of the Drum   30
    Heart Rate and Blood Pressure   32
    Healthy Heart Rate   33
    The Resounding Beat   34

3.   VIBRATIONAL ENERGY   39
    Vital-bration   39
    Frequencies Seen and Felt   40
    Healing Vibes   43
    Energetic Anatomy   45
    Food, Sleep, and Good Energy   46
    Sympathetic Resonance   48
    Synchronicity   49
    The Capacity for Empathy   51
    Energetic Consciousness   53

4.   SOUND ENERGY
    Mother Nature's Powerful Resonators   59
    The Physics of Sound   60
    Psychoacoustics   62

	The Mechanics of Hearing Sound	63
	Prana and the Flute	64
5.	THE MUSIC CONTAINER	71
	The Human Need for Music	71
	Music in Utero	73
	Music and the Brain	75
	Music and Emotion	77
	Music Soothes the Sympathetic	79
	Musical Entrainment and Attunement	80
6.	THE ROOTS TO OUR RHYTHM	88
	Musical Identity	88
	Musical Tendrils	90
	The Tree	92
	Putting Down Roots	94
7.	THE HEART OF OUR ANCESTORS	99
	Lines in the Hand	99
	Attachment and Connection	100
	Welcoming Loving Relationships	102
	Ancestral Cords	103
	The Lives We Never Knew	105
	Trauma in the Brain and Body	107
	Creating Our Story	109
8.	HEALING THE ANCESTRAL HEART	115
	Dark Crystals	115
	Honor our Ancestors	117
	Expectations	120
	Nurturing the Inner Child	123
	The Beams of Love	125
	Conceptualizing Home	126
	Awakening Resilience	128
9.	LIVING WITH A CONSCIOUS HEART	135
	The Seat of the Soul	135
	Changing of the Guard	137
	The River of Consciousness	138
	Messages of Affirmation	141
	The Sacred Chant	144

10. THE RADIANT HEART   149
    The Heart's Awakening   149
    Forgiveness   150
    The Sacred Space Within   151
    Deep Listening   152
    Full of Light   153

Idioms of the Heart   159
Epilogue   161
Index   162

List of Creative Exercises

Creative Exercise #1: Heart-Sensory Breathing   9
Creative Exercise #2: Feel Your Heart Dance   22
Creative Exercise #3: Tuning into the Pulse   36
Creative Exercise #4: Heart Card   55
Creative Exercise #5: Musical Pranayama   68
Creative Exercise #6: Musical Life Review   83
Creative Exercise #7: Roots and Trees   96
Creative Exercise #8: Lines in the Hand   111
Creative Exercise #9: Sacred Rituals   131
Creative Exercise #10: Letter to the Self and Other   147
Creative Exercise #11: Gratitude Gift Giving   156

List of Illustrations

Figure 1. *The Yin-Yang Heart* by Amelia Castelli 15
Figure 2. Kenneth Demaine electrocardiogram printout 26
Figure 3. *Untitled Digital Art #1* by David Grey 41
Figure 4. *Untitled Digital Art #2* by David Grey 62
Figure 5. *Interconnected* by Carol Pelletier 74
Figure 6. *Tree #355* by Tamar Reva Einstein 93
Figure 7. *Three Generations Holding Hands* by Krystal Demaine 100
Figure 8. *Ancestral Papers, IV* by Constance Vallis 118
Figure 9. *Guppa's Brain-Heart* by Ezra Demaine 136
Figure 10. *Untitled* by Sara Roizen 154

Acknowledgments

Thank you to all of those who supported and nurtured the development and creation of this book.

Specifically, thank you to Akiko Yamagata for superior copyediting and Danielle Currier for the original and thoughtful cover design - you are both so professional, creative, and steadfast.

Thank you for the beautiful and thoughtful artistic illustration contributions of Amelia Castelli, David Grey, Tamar Einstein, Carol Pelletier, Sara Roizen, and Constance Vallis.

Thank you to those who shared their stories of music and the heart; Sara Roizen, Stan Strickland, Brian Schreck, Constance Vallis, Tamar Einstein, Susan Ridley, Jane Ferris-Richardson, Fred Johnson, Danii Mann, Yousef AlAjarma, Dana Albert-Proos, Phoebe Potts, Jeff Marshall, Rabi Stephen Lewis, Shaun McNiff, Amir Lahav, Gottfried Schlaug, and Chris Newell. Thank you to all of the music makers who played, breathed, moved, and sang with me over the years in music therapy, on the stage, in the classroom, and beyond. Thank you to my music therapy mentors, Louise Montello, Suzanne Hanser, Colin Lee, Peggy Codding, Michael Rohrabacher, and Karen Wacks for the eternal support of my music therapy education and practice. Thank you truly to all of the friends, colleagues, and students who listened to my ideas, read my narratives, and experimented with creative art-making.

Most especially, thank you to my family, my mom Barbara, my dad Kenneth, and my sisters Bridget and Kourtney; when we vibe together there is nothing better.

And to Ezra—my most special musical companion—thank you for your perpetual patience, thoughtful suggestions, artistic contributions, and loving compassion.

Preface

My father taught me that if you can sing it, you can play it. A musician at heart and in life, my father gave me the code to explore my heart's roots and rhythm through music. I began writing this book in 2018 as a reflection on my professional and clinical experiences using the heartbeat as an underlying theme in my work as a music therapist, expressive arts therapist, and yoga teacher. Because of the ebb and flow of life, personal growth, and change, the project evolved beyond its original scope. It became an elaboration on the music of the heart in grief and spirit and contemplation on energetic consciousness. These existential themes came to the fore with my father's unexpected death on New Year's Day, 2019. Listening to the final beats of my father's heart—his eternal, last live music performance—gave me a chance to reflect on the blood within me, the blood that pumps through my own heart, my roots, my lineage, and my individuation.

I ultimately wrote this book to encourage contemplation and as a reminder of the heartbeat as our personal music, our internal rhythm, our backbeat, and the first audio in the soundtrack of our lives. This book asks the reader to consider how music and vibrational energy in the heart can influence our personal story, identity, health, and wellness. Each chapter ends with a song suggestion for companion listening and a reflective art activity. These activities are intended for creative personal processing and meaning-making of the book's narrative; they are not intended to substitute for therapy.

In writing this book, I open my vulnerable and sacred heart to you, the reader; I share my autobiographical accounts in hopes that it gives you the strength to share yours. The most healing thing we can do is begin to tell our story. Music can be the container that can hold our story and listen to it without judgment. It is time to tune into the sacred music of the heart.

The most we can do is to write—intelligently, creatively, evocatively—
about what it is like
living in the world at this time.
—Oliver Sacks, *Insomniac City: New York, Oliver Sacks,*
and Me

Chapter 1

A Call to the Heart

Oh, Friend! There is a treasure in your heart, it is heavy with child. Listen. All the awakened ones, like trusted midwives are saying, "Welcome this pain. It opens the dark passage of grace."

—Rumi

The Heart Is Calling

On January 1, 2019, I laid my head on my father's chest to listen to the last three minutes of the final beats of his heart. This was his final musical expression, and his life's work in music had come to an end. My mom, my sisters, and I took turns listening, resting our head on Dad's chest one last time, between intervals of silence and tears, as we agonized over how this moment could ever be possible. Dad had arrived in the surgical ICU suddenly and unexpectedly, just the night before, after a doctor at our local hospital, told us that he had suffered a subdural hematoma in the right hemisphere of his brain. Dad had been admitted to the local hospital two days earlier after he showed signs of agitation and disoriented behavior. Upon admission, the initial CT did not show any brain lesions, but two days later, after Dad became non-responsive, a second CT scan revealed a massive brain bleed, engulfing all but a small portion of the lower left quadrant of his brain; his corpus callosum (the midline of his brain) had shifted laterally, and his brain stem appeared crushed. The doctor called my mom on New Year's Eve and told her to come to the hospital and to bring her children. The doctor told my mom that Dad was being put on life support and that he would be flown to another hospital so that we could all discuss his surgical options. On New Year's Eve 2018, it was pouring rain, which was a release from the low atmospheric pressure that we had been experiencing for some days prior. My head was raging in sinus pain from the low pressure. My gums ached, my face hurt, and my head pounded. Dad and I had shared knowing that low air pressure triggered our most severe migraines. Dad, in particular, experienced the most debilitating headaches, the kind that would zap his energy, despite migraine meds, and leave him depressed and frustrated, not knowing what to do. No

1

neurologic consultation truly helped my dad with his headaches. However, he was always intrigued by the brain's mechanisms and relished showing me his previous MRIs indicating a cavernous angioma in his left occipital region. The doctors consistently told Dad that the malformation in his brain was nothing of concern and had likely been there since childhood, perhaps passed down along our long lineage of Ashkenazi Jewish ancestors.

When I was doing work in neurologic music therapy and became a research assistant in the Music and Neuroimaging Laboratory at BIDMC /Harvard Medical School in Boston, Dad was particularly interested. He wanted to discuss music and the brain with me. In addition to his neurologic concerns, he also lamented his partial loss of vision due to central serous retinopathy in his left eye. The condition had come on suddenly in 2014 when he was just 60 years old, diminishing his ability to drive a car, read musical notation, and perform jazz music, the heart of his life's creative work. A Berklee College of Music alum, Dad understood how playing music soothes and nurtures the soul. In retrospect, I wonder if there was a correlation between the cavernous angioma and his visual changes—both with origins in the brain's occipital region, which is primarily responsible for vision. On New Year's Day 2019, though, it was not Dad's vision or his heart; it was the brain that caused his fate. On this day, my mom, my two sisters, and I sat together in the family room of the surgical ICU, listening to a team of neurosurgeons and a surgical ICU nurse tell us that no surgical option could offer Dad a meaningful quality of life. His brain was functioning only by a tiny portion of the brain stem—he was only functioning beyond a vegetative state of minimal consciousness. My mom said that Dad would have wanted to be removed from life support to let his beating heart die peacefully, surrounded by his three daughters and his loving wife of 44 years. Dad was the heart of our family. It was his heart that sustained him when his brain failed him. It was his heart that played his final music.

After Dad died, life moved slowly for the next year or so. I felt like I was in a thick haze of fog; it felt sticky, like wading through molasses, one heavy step at a time. My arms felt heavy, my shoes felt stuck to the ground. I began to gain weight, and my once blondish hair started to darken with a few streaks of silver and seemed to turn the texture of straw. I had experienced trauma, and this was how my body responded. When we see someone close to us die, suddenly and unexpectedly, our body can go into shock. Things can feel ungrounded, and unfamiliar; things can seem out of sorts and out of place, including our own bodies. One day at work, as I was walking from my office to my classroom studio, my neck just slumped forward; I could not lift it. It was as if all the muscles in my neck had collapsed. Like a newborn baby, I struggled to hold my head up in strength. My brain processed everything very slowly, almost as if my body and brain were in complete disconnect. I could not wrap my head around the possibility that I would not be able to see my father again, to play our beloved jazz standards together (bass and flute duets), to know that he would be there to help take care of my mom (the love of his life since they were teenagers), or to see what he would look like as an old man. I had a hard time focusing on my work, especially when it came to writing this book because all I wanted to do was write, journal, and create art about Dad. I had informed my expressive therapies undergraduate students of Dad's death and found myself integrating topics of death and dying into many of my classroom lectures and experiences.

During my grief, my heart softened as I slowly opened up to the new emotions and connections sought with my family. All of my years working as a music therapist and consulting in hospice and end-of-life care did not prepare me for the spontaneity of emotional experiences that I succumbed to with the loss of my dad. The process of understanding why and how he died has deepened my own self-reflective heart and the compassionate heart work that I do as a music therapist.

At my father's first yahrzeit, his memorial day, I lit the memorial candle in the little glass jar to burn for 24 hours on the eve of the anniversary of his death, and again on the day of his death, marking and honoring his passing. My mom and my sisters and I, along with our young children, tossed white roses into the ocean in our hometown of Rockport, Massachusetts. We stared in silence as the white flowers gently danced and swayed in the lulling waves. I read a short prayer in place of the Mourner's Kaddish that our rabbi had given us.

> *To the spirits, in whose hands rest the souls of the living and the dead, graciously and mercifully accept my prayer in memory of my loved one, Dad, Grandpa, Guppa, Ken. Remember all of the good and kindly deeds that he did when among the living, grant him peaceful rest, and bind his soul in the binds of life. Exhausted and sanctified to the one who makes peace in the supernal realm, may there be peace for all of the people of all the world.*

At the yahrzeit, I could not tell if it had been a million years or an hour since he had died. Time was playing tricks on my grieving mind. I felt like I was living in a parallel universe, one in which I could imagine only what the other side would convey. Albert Einstein is supposed to have said, "The only reason for time is so that everything does not happen at once." Time is a construct for social navigation. Grief makes me consider if parallel universes exist and if other versions of me exist in another dimension with different paths and different outcomes.

My father was the heart of our family, and his music was what carried a thread of connection with all that he encountered.

Perpetual Music

The heartbeat is the first auditory stimulus that a fetus perceives, and at just 26 weeks in utero, the fetus can begin to hear and respond to its heartbeat (Ullal-Gupta et al., 2013). The beat of the heart is structured, not improvised; it is perpetual and constant, spanning human life until it is the last rhythm produced in our conscious existence. I first became intrigued with the heartbeat rhythm when I was a young music therapy major at Berklee College of Music in Boston in the 1990s. The program had just started in 1996, and I became a first-generation Berklee music therapy graduate. While at Berklee, I took a course called Percussion for Music Therapy with Steve Wilkes, a professor and former Blue Man Group drummer. It was in Wilkes's class that I learned about the heartbeat as fundamental in all cultures—it is the internal beat, the first rhythm that was instructed to the body. In our small class of just five students, we sat on the floor around a gathering drum, which we played with soft mallets made of animal skin and wood. In silent meditation, we tuned into the natural rhythm of our body and our life; and we tuned into what surrounded us. Then, we listened to one another as we played the heartbeat rhythm on that big gathering drum. Wilkes taught us to play naturally with our bodies, to honor the spirit of the drum, and to play from the heart. This was my first experience working and grounding with the heartbeat rhythm, one that I have carried with me for the past 20-plus years on my journey as a music therapist.

The heart provides the human body's most authentic music. It is uninhibited and unstoppable. The heartbeat speaks the rhythm of truth. It is the blood that pumps through the heart, that carries the traumas we may all experience—those unseen memories, thoughts, and fears that build in the autonomic architecture of our body. The blood holds the emotions, the pains, the memories of others and pumps those experiences through the heart, yet it is the heart that gives us a chance at healthful life–a true dichotomy. Uniquely, though, the heart has its own nervous system: the heart feels and senses emotional intuition and sends signals back to the brain. The ancient Egyptians removed the brain during mummification but kept the heart within the body. It was the heart that was considered the organ of reasoning, and therefore there was a greater need for the heart than the brain to continue into the afterlife. Ancient anatomists and philosophers supposed that the heart brought our soul from the spirit world to the body and back again to the river of universal consciousness (Brandt & Huppert, 2021). Ultimately, it is the heart that brings together a community-centered mindset, understanding, and acknowledgment and that is a symbol of love, courage, and kindness, especially in times when the world is experiencing turmoil, transition, grief, and divide.

On the cusp of 2020, a full year after my dad died and when I was so hopeful for the new year to be one of transition and healing, of finding my way through the thinning haze, I found a dying rat in my basement. I was doing laundry when a big, gray rat slowly slinked along the baseboard behind the washing machine. At that moment, I recalled Albert Camus's (1948) book *The Plague*, the part where rats begin to creep out of all of the city's crevices, crawling from sewers and drain pipes and slowly dying for an unknown reason. A few days after I found the dying rat in my basement, I heard of a virus sweeping through China, one that would be called COVID-19 and cause a pandemic that would forever change the face of the world.

This predatory virus transformed itself to eat away at our human social fabric. People quarantined at home. School and work were conducted remotely. Those who could not work from home were furloughed, if not dismissed entirely from employment. Rather than a year of transition and healing, 2020 seemed to be a year of liminal recalibration: very slowly and deliberately pushing the reset button. The pandemic forced humanity to connect to others through our hearts and through virtual reality—we were asked to pause, literally to slow down. To stop going out and stop socializing with others. The human race was asked to consider what can be learned from the pandemic. The news reported that pollution was in decline, the stock markets were crashing, the economy was at a standstill, and many, many people were sick or were dying. At the same time, people were giving back to local communities, spending more time with their children at home, taking walks and getting fresh air, exercising more, meditating more, and showing more gratitude. The common language of human culture came to include the terms *self-isolation* and *social distancing* and the perpetual promise to wear a mask. People were forced to be alone, to be self-reflective. People listened to music as a means to keep comfort, lighten the energy, and enlighten the spirit. The pandemic also caused global societal trauma, one that changed the hearts and minds of those that lived through it. The children who come after this generation, the next cohort, who know the pandemic from the stories of their ancestors, will—with hope—have new insight on socialization, community, and living more fully with heart. While the human race collectively transitions to this new phase of existence, the heart healers who made it through the trauma of the COVID-19 pandemic will carry forever within their bodies the experience and the loss of what occurred.

Entering into Heart Work

Over my years of working as a music therapist, the pulse of the heart has become central to my therapeutic approach. The music therapy iso principle (primary philosophy or one rule) calls upon the therapist to match the music to the patient's mood—to meet a person where they are through musical dynamics and movement. The therapist establishes a musical connection with a patient by matching the patient's rhythm and sound through music making as they play, sing, vocalize, or dance. Once the therapist makes this connection, the music can carry that person to new places emotionally, cognitively, and physically. So clearly and minutely, the meeting place between the therapist and patient in music therapy can reside in the pulse of the heart, an internal physical space that can invite a person to a place of centered conscious awareness. Listening to the heart, tuning inward to the self, and matching the heart's rhythm with an external expression by a drum or similar instrument might allow for a chance to listen to oneself and to be heard by others. I found it a great opportunity to interact with the heartbeat rhythm as a means of connection and communication between music therapist and patient. Regardless of physical or cognitive ability, age, or place, everyone has a heart that can be felt and heard. We can connect to the heartstrings of a person who has died, to our inner child, or to our ancestors from long ago; we can tune inward to our heart pulse and find a place of inner gratitude; we can use the heart rhythm to reduce anxiety and increase oxygen intake; and we can find within the heart our center of healing and truth. The accessible internal pulse of the heart deserves to be nurtured, traveled, discovered, and whole. Spiritual teacher Eckhart Tolle (2004) refers to this kind of nurturance as the sprouting of the seed that comes alive within. He states that we all have knowing within us, connection to others, and deep heart feeling, and it is just a matter of nurturing it.

My music therapy work, coupled with my training as an expressive arts therapist and yoga teacher, has allowed me to find an intermodal arts and wellness practice with a focus on the heart. I draw upon the eight limbs of yoga (Iyengar, 1979), including breath work, movement and posture, concentration, mindfulness, and union, as part of this integrative practice. In my 20s, I completed my first music therapy wellness training with my mentor Louise Montello in Corfu, Greece. At that time, my yoga practice was focused on asana (body) and prana (breath), with an emphasis on fluidity and ease. With my youthfully open heart, my backbends in yoga came easily. Effortlessly, I flopped my body upside down and lifted into an *urdhva dhanurasana* (upward wheel pose) and moved fluidly into a backbend for *dhanurasana* (bow pose); *bhujangasana* (cobra pose) felt like pure bliss. Life was good as a budding music therapist in my 20s, brimming with love for the work I was doing and pouring out true and deep music from the heart with my clients.

Fast-forward to 2012, I was 35 years old, having just completed my yoga teacher training and my PhD in expressive therapies, and I found myself wounded and crawling out of an emotionally and psychologically abusive relationship. The abuse frayed the tender connection with my close-knit family. Trauma blocks our relationship with ourselves and reduces our capacity for true relationships with others. With my once deeply open heart fractured and my neck in pain from leaning too long over a computer to write my dissertation, I learned that I was five weeks pregnant. Even before I learned I was pregnant and while my music making and music therapy work continued to flourish, I began to notice new emotions stirring in my heart-opening yoga poses. Specifically, I felt on the verge of tears in back-bending postures like *ustrasana* (camel pose). With my neck stretched backward, throat completely exposed, heart expanded, and my head facing the person behind me in class, tears streamed from the corners of my eyes. It was as if the tears flooded from my heart and into a deeply authentic emotional pool. Trauma dysregulates the nervous system, and until we free trauma, it will repeat itself until it finds its way out of our body. My body was holding so much trauma and grief and the movement allowed for some release. At that moment, I recognized that my emotional heart had been compromised and that I had lost the heart protection offered by a healthy protective ego (Demaine, 2018). I had stopped observing the events in my life in the way I had once done. I was growing older, and I needed to take better note of my changes and evolutions as a clinician, professor, artist, and soon-to-be mother. I wondered why I had let go of my self-awareness, why I found myself in vulnerable relationships, and why, with all of my training, I was not observing my own heart.

When I recognized that I had not been tending to my own heart, I came to truly realize that the most authentic and vulnerable place we can express from is the heart. It is a place of true awareness.

And at that moment, I was reminded that I needed to start protecting my heart. It is human to be vulnerable. Hinduism and Tantric Buddhism suggest that some of the hallmarks of an overactive heart (or heart chakra) include codependency, saying yes to everything, and a lack of emotional and energetic boundaries (Dale, 2011). Traditional Chinese medicine suggests that emotional trauma and grief can cause heart imbalance. Psychologist and meditation teacher Tara Brach (2016) has said that sometimes we run around not paying attention to things and that the first step is to just take a pause, to recalibrate.

Empowered by my knowledge of self but also feeling fragile, I began to find ways to recalibrate. I started a daily practice of heart-centered breathing and nurturing self-work at home. I found a smart and seasoned psychotherapist to see me every week. I made music, I did art, I wrote in my journal, and I attended prenatal yoga classes twice a week to prepare my body for labor and delivery. I also began to deepen the heart work in my clinical practice by integrating more art, storytelling, writing, and breath work and explored how we hold pain and trauma, both seen and unseen.

Now I am in my 40s, bearing the deep sadness of my father's death and the collective traumas that began in early 2020—social hostility, climate issues, political divide, and a global pandemic–with its own uniquely unfolding trauma. The heartbeat thus has a new meaning, something deeper and more personal, impacting my existential inquiry of the power of the human condition. My father died suddenly and unexpectedly just one year into writing this book. His death was very traumatic, and as we find our way through this kind of trauma, we need to be nurtured. I had been doing work with the heart with music therapy clients and in workshop settings for several years before his death, and I had intended my writing for this project to share solely those creative music therapy experiences. However, I believe that the world calls us to share our stories when they need to be shared. As I share my story, the heart continues to remind me to stay authentic, allow for vulnerability, and explore the sacred meaning of place and space.

I invite anyone whose heart so moves them.
—Rabbi Steven Lewis *(email correspondence, March 10, 2019)*

Companion Listening #1

"This Is a Call" by Foo Fighters (1995)

Creative Exercise #1: Heart-Sensory Breathing

One of the most natural ways to tune into your own heart and ground your awareness to the body is by bringing attention to it through breath and the senses.

Standing or sitting, find a gentle resting position. Breathe in and out finding your natural and easy breath. In your mind's eye, bring awareness to your body by visualizing your position in the space you are sitting or standing. Visualize all the energy surrounding you as it flows in and out of your existence. Notice the temperature in the room, cool or warm; the pressure on your skin, tingling or soft; the sounds, distant or near; the smells, strong or mild; the tastes, sweet or bitter. Recognize that full conscious awareness of your place in the world can be fleeting and momentary, and that acknowledgment of where you are can bring you to the present moment. Time and existence are impermanent, and we are all part of the river of life.

With your body still, your senses alive, and your feet grounded, inhale your hands to your heart center, holding your hands over your heart space, feeling your heart in the palm of your hands. If this doesn't feel welcome, hold your hands by your side or in another relaxing position and visualize breath moving in and out of your heart for the duration of this exercise. Inhale and stretch your arms and fingers upward toward the sky and then exhale your hands to the heart center bringing the freedom of the sky and the warmth of the sun into your heart. In the same fashion, inhale your arms down toward your feet and then exhale your hands back to the heart center bringing grounding into your heart; inhale your arms out to the sides and exhale your hands back to the heart center bringing community and connection into your heart; inhale your arms and hands forward giving gratitude and then exhale your hands back to heart center; finally inhale stretching your arms behind you, releasing anything that doesn't serve you anymore and that you don't want to imprint onto yourself or anyone else, then inhale your hands to heart center, holding the heart dear. Feel your heart's breath, inhaling and exhaling, naturally and freely. Imagine bringing the energy of the environment into your heart, noticing the sensations, the warmth and the cool, the loud and the quiet, and so on. Allow the sensations to linger for a moment and then pass; do this practice once or twice mindfully and presently to bring grounding to an integrative awareness. A silent pulse of energy begins...

9

References

Brach, T. (2016). *True refuge: Finding peace and freedom in your own awakened heart*. Penguin Random House.

Brandt, T., & Huppert, D. (2021). Brain beats heart: A cross-cultural reflection. *Brain, 144*(6), 1617–1620.

Camus, A. (1948). *The plague*. Vintage International.

Dale, C. (2011). *Energetic boundaries: How to stay protected and connected in work, love, and life*. Sounds True.

Demaine, K. (2018). The radiant fire: Confronting the critic and nurturing the inner child. In E. Scholz (Ed.), *Anxiety warrior: Volume two* (pp. 151–162). The Artists Reply.

Iyengar, B. K. S. (1979). *Light on yoga: The bible of modern yoga*. Schocken Books.

Tolle, E. (2004). *The power of now: A guide to spiritual enlightenment*. New World Library.

Ullal-Gupta, S., Vanden Bosch der Nederlanden, V., Tichko, P., Lahav, A., & Hannon, E. (2013). Linking prenatal experience to the emerging musical mind. *Frontiers in Systems Neuroscience,7*(48).https://doi.org//10.3389/fnsys.2013.00048

Chapter 2

The Heart's Occupation

I hope you are blessed with a heart like a wild flower.
Strong enough to rise again after being trampled upon,
tough enough to weather the worst of the summer storms.
And able to grow and flourish even in the most broken places.
—Nikita Gill, *Wild Embers*

Dancing with the Heart

In the English language, the word *heart* contains the words *hear* and *art*. As a metaphor, the heart produces the artful music that we can create within our own bodies through the lub-dub beat. Therefore, the *heart* allows us to *hear* our own *art*.

The first organ to fully develop in the human fetus, the heart provides the fundamental rhythmic beat to all human life. It fulfills the enormous responsibility of keeping all the body's cells alive by pumping about 2,000 gallons of blood each day (Hoag, 2022) through tens of thousands of miles of arteries and veins, all while bringing vitality and oxygen to the body (Cleveland Clinic, 2022). The heart is emotional, it can feel, it can ache, and it can break. The shape of the heart is a symbol that has meaning to humankind across the world. The meaning of love comes to mind when we think of the heart, and it is the heart's chemicals and nerves that give us a chance to feel the most poignantly emotional experiences in human life. With all its complexities, it is the heart that allows us to engage emotional consciousness—the distinctive ingredient to all human life.

The heart conceals itself in the inner walls of the chest cavity, safe from the public eye. We can hear its sounds and rhythms by listening closely, and we can feel its thump and pulse through the veins. In 2017, when I was at a luncheon for a healing arts organization called Express Yourself, I sat next to Stan Strickland, the co-executive director. A jazz musician and dancer, Stan began to tell me about his experiences performing music to his own heartbeat. He recalled, "Because I have a funny heartbeat, the rhythm was asyncopated [without a steady rhythm; out of sync], and it has been one of the most interesting experiences of my life."

11

A couple of years later, I reconnected with Stan to hear more about his heartbeat performances. We talked about how the heartbeat does not always have a steady rhythm or tempo. Heartbeats change in response to stimuli, emotions, temperature, illness, or position. Performing to his own heartbeat, Stan said, was an idea of his friend Christopher Janney, a composer and architect who had become known for creative sound installations in major sites like airports and performance halls. In 1978, after Janney's father had died of a heart attack, he became interested in how the heartbeat could inform his creative work. Janney began to involve dancers and incorporate heartbeat recordings in his live performances. He used a mobile remote monitoring device, which did not have to be attached to a dancer and allowed for greater freedom of movement. Janney's heartbeat performances were presented in many locations and included notable choreographers, dance companies, artists, and musicians (Koeppen, 2013). Stan recalled performing with Janney at Lincoln Center Plaza in New York, outside of Symphony Hall in Boston, and at the entrance of Disney World in Orlando.

Performing to the sound of his own audible heartbeat, Stan improvised dance, movement, and singing, while sometimes playing the saxophone or the flute. He experimented with doing push-ups while performing, and sometimes playing bebop, then at some point, he would lean over and start playing "My Funny Valentine" on the saxophone—and then slowly rise. The movement of Stan's body changed the tempo of his heartbeat, which in turn changed the way he played the instrument, sang, and vocalized. He commented that although the heartbeat's irregularity makes it difficult to play music in time, "Once you get your body to a certain place, your heart stays at a certain place." He discovered that when he contracted his diaphragm, his heartbeat sped up, and if he put his head lower than his hips, the tempo slowed down. He could change the choreography to his own tempo with his body movements. When he was playing his instrument, he had to keep his abdomen contracted if he wanted to maintain a certain speed. During the performances, a cardiographic display of his heart's electrical activity was projected on a screen—but the performance design focused mainly on the sound of the heart, coming through the speakers.

While Stan and Janney's performance collaborations were novel at the time, others were also interested in the heart for performance reasons. The creative percussionist Milford Graves, in the documentary film about his life and work, *Milford Graves Full Mantis* (Meginsky, 2018), talked about his heartbeat studies, which began when he found medical audio recordings of heartbeat rhythms and became fascinated with the tonality of the sound. In the 1960s, Graves pursued a year of study at the Eastern School for Physicians in New York City, where he worked in a veterinarian research lab examining blood and tissues. He spent his lunch breaks browsing at Barnes and Noble Bookstore, and one day, looking in the cardiology section, he found a recording of *Stethoscopic Heart Recordings* by George David Geckeler, MD. After listening to the record at home, he called his drummer colleagues to tell them about what he had heard. With a stethoscope and reel-to-reel recorder, he began to document the heartbeats of everyone who came to his house. He heard heart sounds that blew him away—and more sounds than what he had heard on Geckeler's recordings. In 1999, he wanted to further explore heartbeat recordings and purchased an electrocardiogram to record his friends. When Graves listened to the recordings, he began to notice different melodic sounds and tonalities coming from the heart. When he invited his friends over to record their hearts, he told them, "I want to see how you're vibrating inside, how is your body oscillating" (Meginsky, 2020, 31:35). He captured this electrical activity in the body, converted it in a voltage generator, added his own percussive sounds over the beat, and created avant-garde heartbeat jazz. To Graves, each sound has its geometry. The rhythms and sounds generated and inspired by the heart were reminiscent of Graves's percussion performances from the 1960s. The heartbeat taught Graves to explore new sounds, which he continued in his avant-garde performances with dancers across the globe.

The Heart's Meaning

Ancient Greek philosopher and biologist Aristotle (384–321 BCE) described the heart as the center of vitality in the body. In his early dissections of animal hearts, Aristotle observed that the heart is a strong and thick muscle, tightly woven and filled with heat, that distributes heat and blood to other organs. Aristotle presumed that when the heart died, the body ran out of heat, blood, and eternal fire, and thus, without the heart, the entire body simply died (Oleksowicz, 2018). Many early scientists thereafter continued to question the heart's true purpose.

The Renaissance polymath Leonardo da Vinci (1452–1519), known among other things for his paintings and his drawings of anatomical, botanical, and paleontological dissections, kept many sketchbooks so that he could teach anatomy through visual architecture. The heart fascinated da Vinci. Most of da Vinci's sketches were based on animals (cows and pigs) and, later, on human bodies. These renderings did not lead to his contemporaries knowing the heart's deeper function; however, because of these detailed studies, viewers were able to understand how the blood is pumped through arteries, veins, and capillaries, which da Vinci noted in the margins of his sketchbook (Cambiaghi & Hausse, 2019). Interestingly, though, da Vinci's anatomical heart drawings were not published until the 1900s and were not even made public until the 1700s as they were too advanced for his time and were long considered too shocking to be widely seen (Sterpetti, 2019).

The heart's sacred shape is recognized widely. For children, the heart is one of the first developmental symbols to emerge in their artistic creations. According to art therapist Jane Ferris Richardson, who specializes in working with children who have been exposed to traumatic life events, the heart shape has intrinsic meaning in human development, and we gravitate toward the image of the heart, drawing it, sculpting it, and forming the shape with our hands (J. F. Richardson, personal communication, June 19, 2020).

In many cultures, the red blood that pumps through the heart is a symbol of love and passion, fire, heat, and sometimes power. In many faith-based traditions, divine energy is received through the heart. Prayer is often conducted with hands at the center of the chest, bringing light and love into the heart. In Christianity generally and Catholicism specifically, the heart is depicted with glimmers of shining gold—a bright sunny light emanating from it. The sacred heart bleeding in compassion for humankind is depicted as a flaming heart radiating divine light. As noted earlier, for the ancient Egyptians, the value of the heart surpassed that of the brain and was central to all knowledge and emotional intelligence. In Chinese culture, it was believed that "the heart was the master of the whole body" (Yu, 2009, p. 114), and in Buddhism, it is believed that the heart is fiery and heats the whole body, which "radiates spiritual thought like a brilliant lamp" (p. 155). One of the first words that I learned as a young girl attending Hebrew School (Jewish Sunday school), was the word *lev*, which means heart; which is considered the home of our intellect. On Yom Kippur, the Jewish day of atonement, the rabbi blows the ram's-horn trumpet, called the shofar, seven times, and the shofar speaks to the heart. Jews wake up the heart on this day, by making a fist and gently tapping or knocking on the chest. My rabbi has told me that this knocking is called the song of songs, in which our beloved is knocking to see if we are there. The knocking on the chest is synchronized with the heart's pulse and resonates with the unseen parts of the heart and the spirit of the universe. The shofar's echo resonates in the heart with the chant *ta-key-ah, shih-va-reem* (S. Lewis, personal communication, February 3, 2020).

The Yin-Yang Heart

The heart's function in the human body is a matter of life and death. Heart function is invariably the cause of death on nearly all death certificates, and aside from the brain-stem function and the respiratory function, the heart is most often the human body's final living organ. When the heart is not functioning properly, the entire human body system is affected.

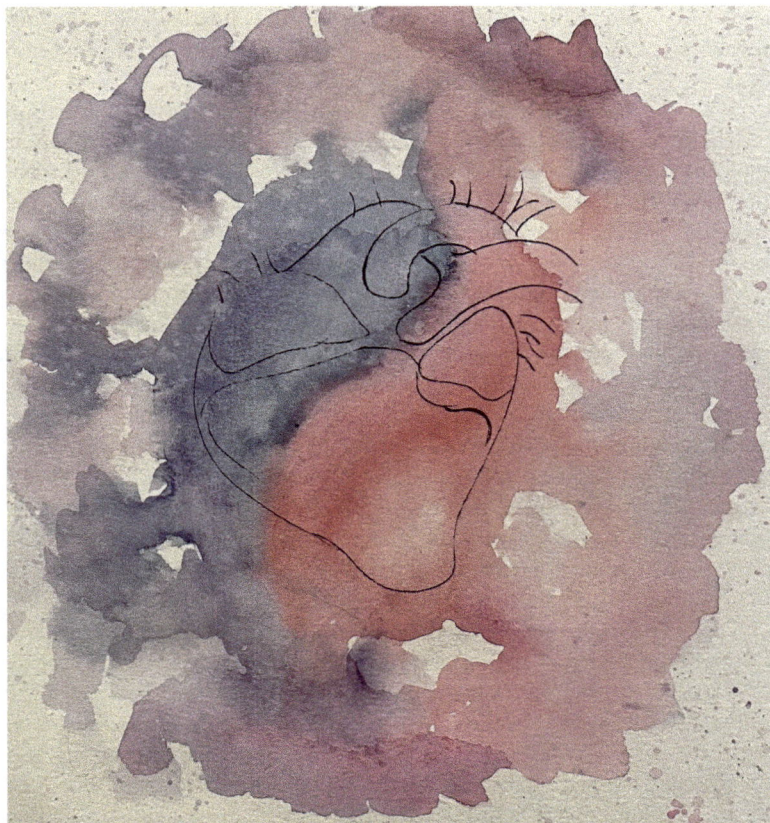

Figure 1. *The Yin-Yang Heart*, 2021. Micron pen and watercolor on paper, 9 x 12 in. Artist: Amelia Castelli. Reproduced by permission from Amelia Castelli.

It has become common to turn to surgical options for an ailing heart. Beginning in the 1960s, doctors started successfully executing human-to-human heart transplant surgeries. Shortly thereafter, the first coronary bypass surgery occurred. In 1982, Barney Clark became famous for being the first recipient of an artificial heart, though he sadly lived for only 112 days afterwards (Eschner, 2016). The heart commonly begins to fail when the arteries get blocked by fat, cholesterol, minerals, or other material, diminishing oxygen intake. Without enough oxygen, the heart's blood vessels can become blocked, and the heart can cease to function. If those vessels cannot be unblocked, new vessels can be grafted in through a bypass. If a bypass is not possible, a complete heart transplant is the only viable alternative. Unlike the brain, which is plastic and can build new neural connections, the heart's cells do not regenerate. Once cells in the heart die, scar tissue develops and function ceases.

The heart, like the brain, has two hemispheres that function independently yet pump blood simultaneously. The right hemisphere is typically represented as the blue side, bringing oxygen-rich blood from the lungs into the heart (illustrated above). The left hemisphere is the red side, pulling blood out of the heart and into the body. The heart moves blood and oxygen around four chambers, pumping in a swirling figure-eight pattern and through vessels and arteries with each beat. The heart with its red and blue blood circulating can be seen in some radiographic ultrasounds as a yin-yang symbol (Lupetti, 2006). In synthesis, the yin and yang together yield a flow of energy, or life force, known in Chinese as qi. Yin represents the dark, feminine, cooling, creative, lunar parts on the left side, while yang holds the bright, masculine, heating, logical, solar elements on the right side. Importantly, the interaction between the parasympathetic (yin) and sympathetic (yang) nerves of the heart work in synchrony, fueling the lungs, brain, and gut, which in turn activates the parasympathetic nervous system to help calm and quiet these organs (Dusi et al., 2020)

The brain's two hemispheres, the parasympathetic (right) and sympathetic (left), are coordinated asymmetrically with body movements, as each brain hemisphere governs the opposite side of the physical body. For example, in music, the conductor holds the baton with the right hand, which is the sympathetic hand, leading and conducting the tempo of the music, representing the masculine, red flame. The left hand is responsible for cueing the musical dynamics, the loud and soft; it is the parasympathetic hand, representing the feminine and cooling. Humans can at times become emotionally "stuck in the sympathetic," or keyed in one place. Just like music, the heart works only when we keep it active, when we keep moving. When people become depressed or anxious or have a sedentary lifestyle, the heart can limit or overextend its function. We should strive for a balance of yin and yang, for homeostasis, for vitality, flow, and function in life. It is important, however, to recognize that polarities and dichotomies exist in all life events. Resistance to and recognition of antagonisms in life give us the skills to walk through the middle of the river where things flow, gracefully and freely, over metaphorical rocks and branches, and through rough-and-tumble places in our lives.

The Emotional Heart

There is a saying: "The heart sees deeper than the eye." Our genetics can determine our health, our lifeline, and our temperament; however, it is the heart that gives us insight and feelings based on our emotions. Many people use *feelings* and *emotions* interchangeably; however, feelings are the subjective meanings we assign to emotions, the six biochemical reactions in our physical body: fear, anger, disgust, sadness, joy, and surprise (Kristenson, 2002). Heart disturbances can be both physically or emotionally induced. According to the Centers for Disease Control and Prevention (2019), cardiac conditions affect about 1 out of every 500 people in the United States and cause 1 out of every 4 deaths. While heart problems commonly have to do with lifestyle, poor exercise, or heart-unhealthy foods, emotional stress can cause cardiac conditions as well. The heart's nervous system is not the source of emotions; however, it is highly responsive to emotional experiences. Both fear (an emotion) and grief (a complex feeling with a myriad of associated thoughts) can cause cardiac injury. The heartbeat can sense distress and trigger sympathetic nervous system responses that put the body into hypervigilant panic mode.

In his TED talk, cardiologist Sandeep Jauhar (2019) states, "Emotions have a direct physical effect on the human heart" (1:05). Jauhar discusses takotsubo cardiomyopathy, also known as broken heart syndrome. Brought on by grief and stress, it results in ballooning in the left ventricle. The first diagnosis was in the 1990s in Japan, and it was so named after its shape, resembling a Japanese clay vessel, with a round bottom and narrowed neck, used to catch octopus. According to Harvard Health Publishing (2022), 90 percent of those diagnosed with takotsubo cardiomyopathy are women aged 58–75. The ballooning of the heart can be seen with an electrocardiogram, and while it usually heals over the course of a month or so, the condition has the potential to cause death or other heart-related diseases. While there are no evidence-based treatments for broken heart syndrome, there are ways to reduce the stress associated with grief.

Takotsubo cardiomyopathy can also be brought on by other kinds of stress. During the COVID-19 pandemic, the international medical journal *QJM* published an article about an 85-year-old woman with no significant past medical history who developed the condition because of stress related to the pandemic (Chada, 2020). It was reported that the woman's blood work and other laboratory tests showed normal results, but the electrocardiogram showed broken heart syndrome. Fortunately, with stress-reduction interventions, the woman recovered within five days.

Trauma-related cardiovascular events can be shocking to the patient, and the sudden and unknown origins of the symptoms can cause additional trauma. In Sweden, researchers studied 136,627 adult men and women who experienced new cardiovascular events and heart disease after trauma and compared their heart health to that of their siblings, who had not been exposed to trauma (Song et al., 2019). The participants' traumas included post-traumatic stress disorder (PTSD), acute stress, and adjustment disorder. The researchers found that cardiovascular disease and conditions were associated with stress and trauma-related situations, even when family history did not play a role. Given the high prevalence of heart-related concerns among people treated in hospitals, medical intake providers need to be skilled in determining if the heart condition is psychologically induced and may be relieved by mental health interventions.

Just as we train the heart physically, such as to reduce blood pressure (discussed in chapter 3), we need to train the heart emotionally as well. When stressful situations occur, a flood of the stress hormone adrenaline, which increases blood circulation and breathing, is released. While a shot of adrenaline can help restart dulled or slowed heart rhythms, too much of the hormone can restrict blood flow to the brain, heart, and other organs. The rush of adrenaline effectively sends a shock to the heart and may overwhelm it, causing sensations similar to a panic attack. Sometimes after psychological traumas, heart palpitations and shortness of breath force people to emergency rooms (Harvard Health Publishing, 2022). People suffering severe anxiety or a panic attack behave quite similarly to people with takotsubo cardiomyopathy, but an echocardiogram will reveal the distinct shape of the ballooning heart, which speaks to the importance of getting a proper diagnosis.

Your task is not to seek for love, but merely to seek and find all the barriers within yourself that you have built against it.

—Rumi

A Heart, a Home, the Nerve

In the motion picture *The Wizard of Oz* (Fleming, 1939), young Dorothy Gale is swept away by a tornado, which lands her in the magical kingdom of Oz. She and her three new friends, the Lion, the Tin Man, and the Scarecrow, all need to find the Wizard of Oz to obtain what they are looking for. In Dorothy's case, it is to return to her home in Kansas. The Lion looks for courage to calm his nerves, the Tin Man, a heart, and the Scarecrow, a brain. On their journey, the four friends link arms and skip down the yellow brick road, singing a song whose lyrics express the search for their desires—a heart, a home, and the nerve.

Recent studies have shown a neurochemical connection between the head, the heart, and the gut, which are all connected through the very powerful vagus nerve (discussed in chapter 8). These three organs contain neurons, commonly known as brain cells. The brain holds about 85 billion neurons, the heart has 40,000 neurons, and the intestines have 100 million neurons. Clinical sources have dubbed these as the "three brains" of the human body because each of these organs has its own nervous system. The gut has five times more neurons than the spinal cord, whose nervous system is referred to as the enteric nervous system.

The gut produces approximately 95 percent of the body's serotonin, a neurotransmitter responsible for mood stabilization, as well as other neurotransmitters that regulate our feelings of happiness (Yano et al., 2015). The heart alone releases the neural chemicals produced by the adrenal glands, which are called catecholamines. This group of chemicals includes norepinephrine (adrenaline), epinephrine, and dopamine, all of which play an important role in the body's fight-or-flight response. As we know from cases of takotsubo cardiomyopathy, the adrenal chemicals released when we are emotionally distressed do result in increased and decreased heart rates. While the heart is neurologically and chemically the ruler of our emotions it is the trusting gut and the nervous system that gives the body its intuition. The central nervous system, also known as the autonomic nervous system, connects the lungs, heart, stomach, intestines, bladder, and reproductive organs, which all work in tandem and are in turn informed by our thoughts, feelings, and emotions.

The common notions of relying on our gut, following our heart, or thinking with our sexual organ has scientific backing and are related to the hormones and neurochemicals produced in those regions of the human body. Our neurotransmitters play a role in our emotional regulation, engagement of the autonomic nervous system, and the processing of sensory information. We need to give consideration and respect to the roles of the three brains in our overall health as well as to the corresponding chemicals and hormones that are located in these regions. The three brains create the soul space for the human body. It is all important to listen to your gut, follow your heart, and use your brain.

In *The Wizard of Oz*, however, Dorothy's journey from the Emerald City of Oz and back to Kansas turns out to be just a dream. Our dreams allow us to bring unconscious concerns to a place of conscious awareness. Dreams allow us to reflect and examine how we can resolve what we are looking for. In Dorothy's dream, her friends all need something to be whole. We can see that what the three friends desire and wish for are all inside of Dorothy and are connected to Dorothy's ultimate wish. Once her friends in the dream find the heart, the brain, and the gut, she gets what she is seeking: to be home. We can tune in to our three brains by starting with breath, bringing awareness to our breathing, through our heartbeat, and then noticing the sensations in the belly. The practice of listening to the body by focusing on a single organ brings whole-body awareness and allows us to tap into our internal intuition that gives us information.

Tending to the Heart

Throughout the day, we are given subtle reminders to tend to our heart. We are given these cues maybe through a misstep in the beat, a barely detectable blip on the radar, perhaps an increase in our heartbeat tempo, or another atypical sensation in the heart. This sense to tune in could be emotional, physical, or intuitive. A change of feeling in the heart might offer a reminder to listen more deeply or maybe to go to the doctor and get an electrocardiogram! Our heart can scream out for our attention when it needs us most and can fail us when it does not receive our nurturance. Slowing down, tuning in, and being present by breathing into the heart is a simple exercise and can be just what the heart needs.

We all have hearts, and we can all breathe. Each time we inhale and exhale, we reoxygenate the blood that pumps through the heart. We take care of our heart from the inside out by eating well, exercising, and reducing stress in our lives. We can also nurture our heart by tuning into our body and listening. Tending to the heart is a method of tending to the most important relationship in our lives—our relationship with ourselves. Listening to the heart is hard work, just as it can be challenging to listen to the places that resist our love. Paying attention to your heartbeat, to every pulsation, to every movement you make is an act of loving kindness to the self.

The heart is a muscle. Just like any other muscle in our body, the heart requires exercise and attention for good health. We know the importance of exercise in maintaining the physical structure of muscles in our body—we tone our biceps and triceps, our legs muscles and abs, to feel strong and stay fit. Getting cardiovascular exercise builds the heart muscle, strengthening it to pump blood. Exercising our skeletal muscles, attached to the bones of our body, intrinsically massages and exercises the heart, simply through the act of physical movement.

Kirtan singer Krishna Das (2020) says there is power in having an inner smile—within the heart—one that is sacred and unseen yet can radiate and give strength to the vital organ of the heart. Kirtan is a yoga practice of chanting and singing devotional Hindu mantras with divine names. When each mantra is sung, it is intended to resonate with a different vibration. Krishna Das chants through the accompaniment of an organ-like keyboard instrument known as the harmonium, a melodic traveling instrument. Das says that the names of the divine that he chants are names that exist within us; saying the names is powerful and moves us closer and deeper into ourselves and to who we truly are. Repetitive chanting of kirtan brings a visceral feel and aliveness to the body, as the mantras are sung freely, to bring a person to a present moment. Das calls this moment of presence while singing kirtan a "letting go," one that helps us release all of the negative stories that we tell ourselves, that color our lives, our days, and our relationships. Around 2001 I attended a very packed and lively Krishna Das concert at the Berklee Performance Center in Boston. Das sat in the middle of the stage on a Persian rug with his legs crossed, as he chanted livelily, told stories, and played the harmonium. The audience listened, sang along, and danced vivaciously–which felt spiritual to me and seemed to transcend the entire space, almost as if I was in a different world from the bustling streets of Massachusetts Avenue just outside of the theater doors. Das's concerts are known for being vibrant and upbeat. People come to Das's concerts to be part of a community, to transcend the moment, to be within good vibes, to dance, sing, be free, and let go without judgment. We can become victims of our own stories. We so often let the outer world destroy our inner happiness. Giving ourselves unconditional love and understanding can help to release those stories. We need to bring more ease and understanding into our lives through kindness and compassion for ourselves and others. We all have this ability within our hearts for true presence, and that presence can be uncovered through kirtan's devotional vibrational singing. Music nurtures the heart through its positive energy, its rhythmic vibrations, and its soothing calm. If we can take a moment to sit and breathe with music, we can give our heart the chance to tune into the calming vibrations that surround us. As my son once told me, "Listen to the light inside of you, the light of your heart."

Krystal L. Demaine

Companion Listening #2

"Let's Dance" by David Bowie (1983)

Creative Exercise #2: Feel Your Heart Dance

At any time of the day and in any location, we can tune into the changes in the heart rhythms. Place your hand on the left side of your chest over your heart. Throughout the day, notice how the heart changes when you listen to certain music, drink caffeine, or see someone you love. We can listen to our beat and the space between the beats; time can seem to slow down. We can become lost or entranced in the steady ostinato pattern. We can exaggerate each moment to give voice to each movement of the body. Notice how your body movements change with different types of music; notice how your heart rate and breath rate change in response to that different music. The heart's tempo can increase when the nervous system is activated. When the sympathetic nervous system is engaged, in a moment of fear or anxiety, our heart rhythm increases, pulsing more beats per minute. When we are in anxiety-provoking environments, our body responds accordingly, from our heart's center. When the parasympathetic nervous system is activated the heart rate slows, the breath slows, and adrenaline decreases . . . Feel your heart dance to the external musical environment.

My spirit finds a quiet home in the peace of my heart. I take the time to shift my awareness there. Feeling strong, rhythmic beat of my heart, I slow down my thinking and smooth out my emotions. The faster the world seems to move, the more I can maintain and sustain my own inner serenity by making this conscious choice.

—Psalm 46:10

References

Cambiaghi, M., & Hausse, H. (2019). Leonardo da Vinci and his study of the heart: A 500-year anniversary appreciation of a maestro. *European Heart Journal, 40*(23), 1823–1826.

Centers for Disease Control and Prevention. (2019, December 9). *Heart Disease: Cardiomyopathy.* https://www.cdc.gov/heartdisease/cardiomyopathy.htm

Chada, S. (2020). "Covid-19 pandemic" anxiety-induced Takotsubo cardiomyopathy. *QJM: An International Journal of Medicine, 13*(7), 488–490.

Cleveland Clinic. (2002). *How does blood flow through your body.* *https://my.clevelandclinic.org/health/articles/17059-how-does-blood-flow-through-your-body#:~:text=This%20vast%20system%20of%20blood,through%20your%20body's%20blood%20vessels.*

Das, K. (2020, May 2). *Enter into the heart through chanting practice with Krishna Das: A kirtan musical experience to find loving presence and peace of mind* [Workshop presentation]. Krishna Das Events.

Dusi, V., De Ferrari., G., & Mann, D. (2020). Cardiac sympathetic-parasympathetic interaction: The endless story of yin and yang. *Journal of the American College of Cardiology: Basic to Translational Science, 5*(8), 811–814.

Eschner, K. (2016, December 2). Remembering Barney Clark, whose ethically questionable heart transplant advanced science. *Smithsonian Magazine.* https://www.smithsonianmag.com/smart-news/remembering-barney-clark-whose-ethically-questionable-heart-transplant-advanced-science-180961271/

Fleming, V. (Director). (1939). *The Wizard of Oz* [Film]. Metro-Goldwyn-Mayer (MGM).

Harvard Health Publishing. (2022, May 19). *Takotsubo cardiomyopathy (broken-heart syndrome).* https://www.health.harvard.edu/heart-health/takotsubo-cardiomyopathy-broken-heart-syndrome

Hoag. (2022). *Heart basics.* https://www.hoag.org/specialties-services/heart-vascular/conditions/heart-basics/#:~:text=It%20pumps%20blood%20continuously%20through,about%202%2C000%20gallons%20of%20blood.

Jauhar, S. (2019, July). *How your emotions change the shape of your heart* [Video]. TEDSummit 2019. https://www.ted.com/talks/sandeep_jauhar_how_your_emotions_change_the_shape_of_your_heart?language=en

Koeppen, B. (2013, February 19). *Insights from the composer of "HeartBeat" Christopher Janney, to be performed at 2013 DC Heart Ball*. Washington Exec. https://washingtonexec.com/2013/02/insights-from-the-composer-of-%E2%80%9Cheartbeat%E2%80%9D-christopher-janney-to-be-performed-at-2013-dc-heart-ball/

Kristenson, S. (2022, April 21). *Emotions vs feelings: 7 important differences*. Happier Human. https://www.happierhuman.com/emotions-vs-feelings/

Lupetti, T. (2006). The yin-yang sign. *Radiology, 238*(3), 1070–1071.

Meginsky, J. (Director). (2020). Milford Graves full mantis [Film]. Cinema Guild.

Oleksowicz, M. (2018). Aristotle on the heart and brain. *European Journal of Science and Theology, 14*(3), 77–94.

Song, H., Fang, F., Arnberg, F. K., Mataix-Cols, D., de la Cruz, L. F., Almquist, C., Fall, K., Lichtenstein, P., Thorgeirsson, G., & Valdimarsdottir, U. A. (2019). Stress related disorders and risk of cardiovascular disease: Population based, sibling controlled cohort study. *BMJ, 365.* https://doi.org/10.1136/bmj.l1255

Sterpetti, A. (2019). Cardiovascular research by Leonardo da Vinci. *Circulation Research, 124*(2), 189–191. https://doi.org/10.1161/CIRCRESAHA.118.314253

Yano, J. M., Yu, K., Donaldson, G. P., Shastri, G. G., Ann, P., Ma, L., Nagler, C. R., Ismagilov, R. F., Mazmanian, S. K., & Hsiao, E. Y. (2015). Indigenous bacteria from the gut microbiota regulate host serotonin biosynthesis (PubMed ID No. 2640276). *Cell, 161*(2), 264–276.

Yu, N. (2009). *The Chinese heart in a cognitive perspective: Culture, body, and language*. Mouton de Gruyter

Chapter 3

It Starts with the Pulse

How beautiful to find a heart that loves you, without asking you for anything,
but to be ok.

—Kahlil Gibran, *The Prophet*

The Eternal Rhythm of the Heart

We begin life's journey with the pulse—the heart's eternal rhythm. Like waves on the ocean, the undulating flow of blood pulsating through the veins and arteries is what gives the heart its perpetual beat. With its ostinato pattern keeping the tempo, the pulse becomes our home base, a familiar place to return to and rest. In music therapy, I begin group sessions by inviting participants to feel the pulse inside themselves. This pulse is sacred music in one's body. In music therapy and yoga, I relate the pulse to *home*—the grounding space inside the self, a place to return to when we become out of touch, lost in the other beats and rhythms that may surround us. With hands over the heart-space, I invite each person to find their own way to find their pulse. Some choose to place the index and middle finger on the cardioid artery, to the right or left of the windpipe, feeling the blood pump from the heart up to the head, face, and neck; others begin palpating the radial artery at the bones in the wrist, closest to the thumb. The sensation may perhaps, if it feels safe, take us back to the primal eternal heartbeat, to the womb, connecting to the first rhythm of our lives. Whether that womb is dear or lost, it very well may be our first imprint in vibration and rhythmic sensation. I ask the group to listen to the lub-dub, lub-dub, lub-dub created by the heart's chambers and valves opening and closing, bringing us to our center and our own sacred, internal home. When we are in deep silence, when all other auditory stimuli fade away, the heart's beat is the only sound to remain.

As my father lay in his hospital bed, in a near-vegetative state, on New Year's Day 2019, my family did not know how much he could hear the sounds around him, receive our touch, or consciously understand the events that were playing out. A social worker approached me, my mom, and my sisters with a printout of Dad's electrocardiogram (shown below). This little curled-up strip of paper, showing a black-and-white schematic of the electric impulses so painlessly, simply, passing through his heart, landed in my hands. It felt eternal and sacred. The contour of the pulsation, prosodic in nature like music, rang out a visceral melody, just like how he played his bass guitar, so strong and crisp—his thumping walking bass line when he played Sly and the Family Stone's "Thank You for Letting Me Be Myself Again" and "Donna Lee," played with terse articulation like Jaco Pastorius. I wanted to hear my father in all of his vibrational energy, his internal song, for one last musical expression. His heart echoed his spirit, his soul, and his musical essence through that pulse on the cardiogram, the one rhythm that could hopefully soothe me, my mom, and my sisters again.

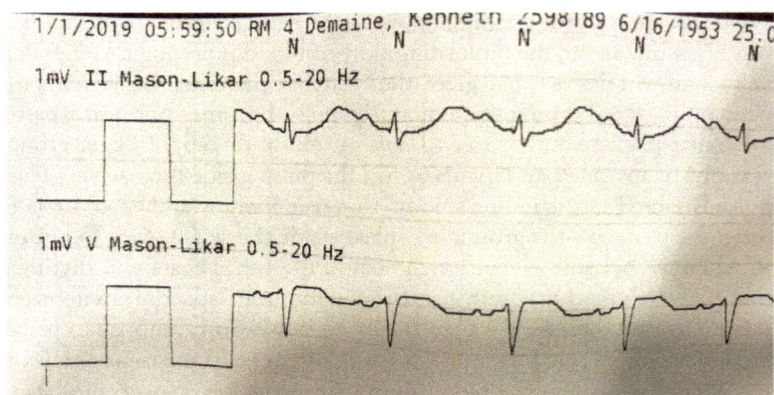

Figure 2. Kenneth Demaine electrocardiogram printout, January 1, 2019.
Courtesy of Lahey Health.

Can you imagine the sound of your heartbeat as your eternal music? Your marching rhythm, your energetic life force, your forever music. The pulse is our primal neonatal audible expression and our earliest visible movement. In 2001, I was given a music therapy referral for a seven-year-old girl with a rare genetic disease that caused delayed growth, seizures, intellectual disability, visual impairment, and muscle spasticity. Because of the disease, her muscles and organs were also highly prone to infection, which made her life span undetermined. Her mother received the diagnosis while she carried her daughter in utero, and with music in mind, she reached out to her brother, a professor of music with experience recording fetal heartbeat rhythms. Her mother shared this story with me when I was doing the initial intake for music therapy. She told me that her brother held his microphone on her belly to record the fetal heart sounds in her womb. In doing so, this internal beat of her daughter's heart had become deeply cherished as a living musical sound that will live on. This heartbeat is her daughter's living music.

Recording the Sacred Heartbeat

The once-novel practice of recording the fetal heartbeat has become so popularized that there are even cell phone applications that anyone can use to make fetal heart recordings. For example, Womb Beats can record up to 12 minutes of a fetal heartbeat through the microphone on a cell phone held up to a pregnant belly. The ebb and flow of the fluid in the womb and the muffled beating of the heart, like white noise, have been found to soothe babies in utero, put them to sleep, reduce their anxiety, and lower their heart rate (Rand & Lahav, 2014). These sounds are the first auditory imprint from the mother's body and give natural comfort. After a baby is born, parents can play with the sounds of their own baby's in utero heartbeat to support the child's transition from the womb.

In 2007, while navigating my path into a doctoral program, I met with my mentor, Suzanne Hanser at Berklee College of Music. Dr. Hanser introduced me to Amir Lahav, who at the time was doing a postdoctoral fellowship in the Music and Neuroimaging Laboratory. Lahav was using functional magnetic resonance imaging to observe the neural activity of typical adults while they listened to piano melodies (Lahav et al., 2007). They looked specifically at a region of the brain responsible for the auditory-motor feedback loop, known as the arcuate fasciculus. Lahav's work assessed how playing and listening to music activates Wiernecke's area (responsible for comprehension and processing of written and spoken language) and Broca's area (responsible for the expression of written and spoken language). Activation in these brain regions indicated that even when simply listening to a learned melody or its variation, the brain behaved as if it were either playing the melody or trying to make sense of it. This is the brain's instinct to process musical sounds as language. Learning of these neural correlations between music and language processing deepened my interest in the music therapy work I was doing with nonverbal children with autism. That work related specifically related to empathy and how we relate to and understand one another through our human tendency to establish affinities.

After Lahav finished his postdoctoral work, he shifted populations to work with premature babies through Brigham and Women's Hospital in Boston. In 2015, Lahav and his colleagues tested to see if exceptionally premature babies, some born at just 25 weeks, could catch up to normal development if they listened to heartbeat sounds paired with the mother's voice. Babies born before full gestation tend to have a lag in language acquisition, neurologic function, and motor development compared with babies born at full term. Lahav and his colleagues (Webb et al., 2015) worked with 40 babies and their mothers; 19 served as a control group and received routine care in the neonatal ICU, and 21 received the described listening intervention along with routine care. Each mother in the listening group was recorded reading the story *Goodnight Moon* and singing "Twinkle, Twinkle, Little Star." The researchers also used a stethoscope to record the mother's heartbeat. While in their warm incubators, the 21 newborn preemies in the intervention group listened to their mother's voice and heartbeat three times a day for 45 minutes each time. The listening took place over one month. After 30 days, neuro-ultrasound images found that the babies who listened to their mother's singing and reading along with her heartbeat sound had a larger auditory cortex (the area of the brain that receives and processes sound, voice, and music) than the babies in the control group. A larger auditory cortex typically results in better hearing and language development. The researchers have yet to report on the long-term benefits of this early intervention. But one thing for sure: Lahav and his colleagues were able to give these babies a leg up.

In recent decades, medical doctors have increased their awareness of and attention to music therapy and the heart within medical settings. Both musicians and music therapists have collaborated with doctors to create music with patient heartbeats. The recorded pulse offers tempo, rhythm, and musical accompaniment. Musician and music therapist Brian Schreck, with whom I became friends in the 1990s when we were both students at Berklee College of Music, has an affinity for working with the heart. The "heartbeat music" that Brian creates incorporates patients' heartbeats and allows their families to carry and listen to their loved one's heart indefinitely.

In March 2020, at the start of the COVID-19 pandemic lockdown, I telephoned Brian to discuss more of his heart work. He was in his office at the hospital, but he was not seeing patients. He had to walk through halls covered in medical tape and COVID-19 signs that barred him from doing his beloved work; he had to go directly to his office to do paperwork and other solo projects. His heart broke not to see patients. He told me how he felt lost not doing his music therapy work and not engaging with the heart as he does. I could relate to what he was saying as many music therapists identify their passionate soul work as making music with people, not alone.

Brian's heart work began as a music therapist working in the neonatal ICU, trying to find ways to connect with prematurely born babies, many of whom have congenital heart defects. He started by improvising lullabies with the families while the babies were being intubated or sedated. Then, one day, while watching the television program *Good Morning America*, he saw the emotional story of a woman who donated her son's heart after he had unexpectedly died in a skiing accident. The recipient of her son's heart was a young girl. A year after the transplant, the woman met the girl and her mother. The mother, a nurse, put a stethoscope on her daughter's heart and the ear buds on the woman so that she could hear her son's heart beating once again. Brian was deeply moved by this story and used it as a reminder that we need to use the heartbeat as a sound in music therapy.

In Brian's work, recording the heartbeat allows him to preserve the human experience for his patients, many of whom have life-limiting illnesses. He also records families laughing, talking, joking, or making whatever other sound they are in that moment. Brian learned how integral recording sessions can be to patient treatment while he was completing his master's degree in music therapy at the Nordoff-Robbins Center for Music Therapy at New York University. Clive Robbins, the cofounder of the center and cocreator of the Nordoff-Robbins approach to music therapy (NordoffRobbins, 2008), taught Brian to always record patient sessions because they can always be used; everything can be used. This person-centered approach requires that all sessions be recorded, which allows the therapist to self-critique and provide a more accurate assessment of client progress. For Brian, it was not just his clients' actions or behaviors during music therapy that needed to be recorded for his learning. He noticed there was another quieter space that deserved to be recorded—the heart.

When something catastrophic happens to a baby in utero, the mother can be referred to perinatal hospice. For an expectant mother who may be delivering a stillborn child, the recorded heartbeat is the only sound that mothers will be able to hear from their baby. Many preterm babies do not survive, and those that do live function at various stages of neonatal development. The death of a baby at any stage of development is a deep and significant loss to the mother and her family and therefore must be appropriately honored and grieved. In Brian's work, he attends obstetric appointments with expectant mothers preparing for nonliving births. He says, "In the waiting room, people would be happy in anticipation of their newborn child, but unaware of the silent burden that [my] clients were carrying" (B. Schreck, personal communication, March 15, 2020). Brian's role is to be supportive, and he is there to record the ultrasound and to allow the expecting mother the time to cherish moments with her child. He uses the recorded sound to create anything the mother or family wants, whatever honors the life experience.

Brian records fetal heartbeats using a few stethoscopes with a lavalier microphone attached to the inside. The microphone plugs directly into his laptop so that he can amplify and record the source. Brian also uses the Eko DUO application, which provides an electrocardiogram readout from the stethoscope source. Through this setup, he can record the audio and the schematic printout.

Like many music therapists, Brian works with people across the life span, from infants to older people, and finds his approach resonates with all ages. A teenager originally not interested in music therapy explores making a beat with their own heartbeat. Sampling the heartbeat audio, overlaying rhythms with a drum machine or a prerecorded song, or adding newly composed lyrics or sounds over the heartbeat, can be a meaningful way for a teen to engage in creative music making. Adults with cancer might create a recording of themselves singing over their heartbeat. By giving the recording as a gift, they can give a loved one a memory of their life that may forever be cherished.

When someone dies and we have a recording of their heartbeat, we can continue, in theory, to hear and engage with that person. The heartbeat allows us musically to continue to collaborate with the energy and spirit of someone who is no longer alive. What I learned in Steve Wilkes's percussion for music therapy class is that the heartbeat is eternal and sacred. Even though we did not discuss recording the heartbeat in his class, we understood that it was important to integrate and be aware of it in our music therapy work. For me, listening to my father's heartbeat, I felt almost like he was telling me that I need to focus on the heart for the remainder of my life's work.

The Pulse of the Drum

One of the most accessible and aesthetic ways to externalize the heart's pulse is to play the beat on a resonant drum. Many cultures have regarded the drum as one of the most healing musical instruments. Used by many traditional healers, the drum accompanies ceremonies from birth to death, reaching the spirit world and beyond. Playing the drum engages the entire sensory system. The proprioceptive sense (joint movement and pressure), tactile sense (touch), and vestibular sense (gravity and balance) are engaged when hitting the drum, whether using the palms or a mallet. Gross arm movements bring a sense of balance and spatial awareness. Joint compression engages the pressure points and sensory processing function to calm and soothe the body. Visceral tingling felt in the fingertips and palms excites the nervous system to a place of balance and sympathetic and parasympathetic symmetry. The entire peripheral nervous system (the nerves that extend beyond the brain and spinal cord) lights up when the body plays the drum (arms moving, ears listening, eyes watching), sending a warm light to the heart and equanimity to the body system.

Traditional drums made of natural fibers like goat or cow skin, wood, and twine, are intended to evoke the spirit of the material it is made of. A traditional drum maker typically begins with the barrel, or the body, of the drum, made traditionally from the trunk of a tree. The wood is carefully hollowed out by hand and measured for balance and dimensional symmetry. Depending on the type of drum, the wooden body has a specific depth to its barrel and thickness to its walls. Some wonderful healing drums include the African djembe drum, the Native American gathering drum, and the buffalo drum, all of which have unique qualities in sound and form. Once the body of the drum is prepared, the drum maker collects an animal pelt to lay over the top of the drum frame. The animal skin becomes the head of the drum. The skin is dried and laid flat, shaved to a smooth touch, and tightened around the top rim of the drum barrel with twine, made of animal gut or grassy fiber. Each animal's skin has its own spirit and own personality depending on the animal and the cultural belief (Horn, 2017).

Holistic health doctor John Diamond (1999) says that when drums play together, it is like a family communicating with each other. In his book, Diamond refers to the drum as a mother: her milk, amniotic fluid, and her womb provide a vessel where the music of our life pulsates, and as the container of all of these elements, the mother is herself a drum that resonates the rhythm. For Diamond, the drum's pulse connects us with our mother and the pulsation of her heart in the womb. The pulse allows our mind, body, and spirit to return to a quiet inward grounding space; and since the term *womb* can be limiting in some of my music therapy work, I often refer to this place as "a safe place within" or "home." As I have noted, to me the pulse is home, not masculine or feminine, but rather a space; when we play the drum, we can be free to express our musical creativity and know that we can return home to the heartbeat rhythm, the pulse.

In July 2020, I had a conversation with Native American drummer Chris Newell of the Passamaquoddy tribe in Maine, and he spoke with me about Northern Eastern Woodland music (C. Newell, personal communication, July 24, 2020). Chris said that he is most happy when he is at the drum. In the circles where he plays, the drum is central and only men play the drum. Dancers, both men and women move around the drum, which resonates and grounds the rhythm of the singing and dancing. The drum is considered a living elder—the grandfather, who must be respected and specially cared for. The grandfather is sacred. Chris said that music makes us want to get up and dance—it is part of the tradition and power that we feel within us—it is the roots of our heart. In the Passamaquoddy tradition, the heart is in the physical body; however, it is the spirit that makes us move, dance, and sing while the heart keeps the tempo.

Heart Rate and Blood Pressure

The true indicators of our health are our heart rate and blood pressure, which give the tempo of our bodies. As a musical term, tempo has to do with how fast or slow the music is performed; this word is also sometimes attributed to other human activities, related to the pace that something is done. When it comes to heart rate and blood pressure, tempo applies only to one. While heart rate deals with how many times the heart beats per minute, blood pressure has to do with the force or pressure of the blood moving through the vessels (the tubes or chambers that carry blood to and from the heart). According to the American Heart Association (2022), an increased heart rate does not always correspond with increased blood pressure. For example, when we exercise, our heart rate increases or has a quicker tempo, but that may not play a role in the pressure.

Blood pressure is represented by two numbers, indicating systolic and diastolic pressures and which can range from normal, elevated, to hypertensive, stages 1, 2, and 3, respectively. The first number indicates systolic pressure, which is exerted by the heart. The systolic number typically ranges from 90 to 120. The second number indicates diastolic pressure, or the pressure exerted through the arteries (tubes connecting to the heart) between heartbeats. This number typically ranges from 60 to 80. You can think of systolic as the whole heart system and diastolic as the dials or arteries that connect to the system. Generally, blood pressure increases as we grow older. Infants have considerably lower blood pressure compared with adults, and boys' blood pressure is generally a bit higher than girls' (Reckelhoff, 2001).

A healthy adult's resting heart rate is 60–80 beats per minute (bpm). Well-trained athletes generally have a slower resting heart rate, closer to 40 bpm; further, athletes are better able to bring their heart rate down to normal than those who do not regularly exercise. Young children typically have a faster heart rate than adults, and newborn babies have even faster heart rates at 100–150 bpm. A child's heart rate is faster to keep up with their quick metabolism. Children ages 3–4 can have a range of 80–120 bpm, which progressively decreases as they child grow older. At around 10–12 years of age, a child's heart begins to fall in the adult range of 60–80 bpm (van den Berg et al., 2018). Fetal heart rate, detected by sonogram at just six weeks, can range from 110–160 bpm. It gradually increases at around 10 weeks in utero and then decreases again to around 130 bpm at about 40 weeks in utero, or when the baby is at full term (Gebuza et al., 2018).

Healthy Heart Rate

In general, a lower heart rate may indicate better health, while overexerted hearts may beat faster. Overexertion of the heart, caused by fatty blood or stress, has been found to decrease life span and reduce the quality of life. On the other side of the coin, a heart rate that is too low may cause fatigue, dizziness, or fainting. While exercise increases heart rate, it also reduces resting rate, the rate at which we live in our daily lives. Moderate exercise such as walking, yoga, and dancing; healthy eating, possibly with a vegetarian diet; and pleasurable stress-reducing activities like creative writing, music, or art making have been shown clearly to improve overall wellness, including heart health (Hanser 2016; Montello, 2002). As Herbert Benson (1975) describes in his groundbreaking *The Relaxation Response*, when Harvard researchers studied people who engage in Transcendental Meditation, they found these individuals had decreased heart rate, metabolic rate, and breathing rate. Various meditation exercises can be done to achieve such the relaxation response, which is further discussed later. As we become healthier by practicing wellness activities and eating nutrient-rich foods, the heart operates more efficiently as it pumps blood. In addition to lifestyle choices, age, activity level, mood, body size, medications, and one's living environment can impact heart rate and blood pressure.

Some research has suggested that a person has a finite number of heartbeats in a lifetime. An article published in the *British Journal of Medicine* in 2013 found that over a 16-year longitudinal study with 5,200 men, higher pulses directly correlated with a shorter life span (Jensen et al., 2013). The research also found that increased heart rate caused by stress or trauma often leads to cardiovascular disease. Along similar lines, a public database called the Heart Project (The Public Science Lab, 2020) shows that a healthy heart is a key to longevity. The project has tracked the life of various animal species and the number of heartbeats recorded in each group over an average lifetime. The Heart Project has concluded that all mammals get about one billion heartbeats over the course of a lifetime. The number of beats, of course, depends on the same heart-health factors discussed earlier. According to the Heart Project, the average human experiences about two billion heartbeats (pre-COVID-19) during their life span.

The Resounding Beat

In the children's book *Heartbeat* by Evan Turk (2018), the author illustrates the perpetual resounding beat of the heart, like the ebb and flow of sea currents, through the story of a mother whale and her calf. The key illustration in the story shows a whale's heart pulsating a resonance of concentric waves, like visible sonar in the deep ocean. They are two heartbeats swimming in the deep blue sea, a mother and her calf. "One song, one heart," Turk says. The steady underlying rhythm of the heartbeat illustrates the eternal cadence of the pulse that connects us all. The connection created through others by vibration reminds us how we are healing together, nurturing from the inside out.

In my practice, when I work with children with intensive special needs, the group gathers to the physical beat of the heart. Children come to the circle in wheelchairs; they stand supported by mobility contraptions moved along by their teachers and nursing staff. I begin to play a deep bass pulse on my Bahia Buffalo Black Earth drum, slowly, about 50 bpm. As my mallet thumps and resonates its rich, deep tone on the drum head, I begin to chant the words "heartbeat, heartbeat, heartbeat." I ask the children and their teachers to bring hands to the heart, to breathe, to calm down, maybe close their eyes, and chant with me. Some can move their arms to their hearts with assistance and some staff brings their own hands to the children's hearts, and everyone does something. Children who have arrived at the group anxious or crying and maybe uncertain about what the group would offer seem to become grounded, breathe, and settle in. The nurses tell me that the children show decreased blood pressure, increased pulse oxygen levels, and relaxed arms and postures. The collective resonant vibration permeates each student, almost as if showering the group with a sense of unity and equanimity.

The heart's pulse maintains the flow of vital information exchanged throughout the body. The pulse roots us through the blood to the rhythm of our many, many ancestors, to whom we are all connected and who can maybe bring us some support. The pulse can bring us to a deep place for reconciliation, confrontation, connection, and inner inquiry; it can bring us home and back to the concentric vibrational waves of our environments near and far. At every medical appointment, the first three things examined are the heart rate, blood pressure, and pulse oxygen level. Assessing rhythmic regularity and healthy heart rate is key. Listening to the heart offers us a journey into an eternal rhythm and toward exploring what we want in life—to be actualized in self. By looking inward, we can see the truth of self and honor the sacred space within. This deep listening is a method of tuning into our own internal music. Listening to the heart is time well spent because it gives you time with your body—a time to rest, recalibrate, and nurture.

So much can happen in a single heartbeat. Perhaps if we deepened our thoughts and feelings, perceiving each heartbeat moment as a sacred moment, we could find greater attunement to sense the minute rhythms of life. Perhaps we could consider each inhalation and exhalation as a metaphor for birth and renewal, and perhaps with each breath, we could find a release of pain, a transformation from our fears, and a place of freshness. Acknowledging the depth of feeling in each moment as a sacred gift may allow us to find higher value in the lackluster. As you read these words, many beats of time, pulses of existence, have tiptoed by. Each rhythmic beat of your heart, your forever and personal music, is what carries you through this life cycle. The concise and calibrated event of a single heartbeat requires an intake of blood coordinated with valves opening and closing. Without the functions of the heart, the remaining organs (such as lungs, kidneys, and brain) would cease to function. It all comes down to the single heartbeat, whose continuance sustains these activities.

My father's cardiogram, with the simple pulsations, reminds me of how delicate and precise the pulse is. To nurture the pulse is to nurture the soul and to keep our own internal music pulse sacred for years and years to come. Lub-dub, lub-dub, lub-dub . . .

Companion Listening #3

"Eclipse" by Pink Floyd (1973)

Creative Exercise #3: Tuning into the Pulse

The mindful exercise of tuning into the pulse brings awareness of the heart and the blood that pumps through the body; it also brings acknowledgment that our blood was once pumped in our ancestors. When doing this exercise, you are not expected to sit for a long time or conjure any images intentionally. Rather, you are invited to just allow yourself to sit quietly, feel your pulse, and send gentle understanding to the blood that pumps withink you. If you have a drum, have it close by. Hand drums such as the frame, buffalo, djembe, or tubano drum well suit this activity.

Locate the pulse point you prefer to feel or palpate. You can palpate the pulse by gently touching one of your pulse points with your first and middle fingers. The easiest points to locate are at the carotid artery, next to the windpipe, or at the radial artery, next to the wrist bones. Once you feel the pulse, entrain to its tempo in your mind. Count the pulses silently and internally, and once you have a grounded sense of the count, begin to externally tap out the pulses on the drum in front of you. Once you a sense of playing your pulse on the drum, you have the freedom to move from or play around the steady beat as you wish on the drum. Be free and be unique. When you feel the desire to come to your home base, your pulse, do so. Maintain the original pulse on the drum for a moment until it fades away and then sit quietly for a moment. In silence, notice the sensations or residual musical vibrations in your hands, your belly, and your heart. Notice if you were able to play around your original internal pulse, play freely, and then come back to your home base. Notice how it felt to be free from the original pulse and play uniquely. Notice how it felt to come home to the original internal pulse of the heart.

References

American Heart Association. (2022). *Blood pressure vs. heart rate (pulse)*. https://www.heart.org/en/health-topics/high-blood-pressure/the-facts-about-high-blood-pressure/blood-pressure-vs-heart-rate-pulse

Benson, H. (1975). *The relaxation response*. Harper Torch.

Diamond, J. (1999). *The way of the pulse: Drumming with spirit*. Enhancement Books.

Gebuza, G., Saleska, M., Kazmierczak, M., Mieczkowska, E., & Gierszewska, M. (2018). The effect of music on cardiac activity of a fetus in a cardiotocographic examination. *Advances in Clinical Experimental Medicine, 27*(5), 615–621.

Hanser, S. (2016). *Integrative health through music therapy: Accompanying the journey from illness to wellness*. Palgrave Macmillan.

Horn, G. (2017). *Spirit drumming: A guide to the healing power of rhythm*. Sterling Publishing Company Incorporated.

Jensen, M., Suadicani, P., Hein, H, & Gyntelberg, F. (2013). Elevated resting heart rate, physical fitness and all-cause mortality: A 16-year follow-up on the Copenhagen male study. *British Journal of Medicine, 99*(12), 882–887.

Lahav, I., Saltzman, E., & Schlaug, G. (2007). Action representation of sound: Audiomotor recognition network while listening to newly acquired actions. *The Journal of Neuroscience, 27*(2), 308–314.

Montello, L. (2002). *Essential musical intelligence: Using music as your path to healing, creativity, and radiant wholeness*. Quest Books Theosophical Publishing House.

NordoffRobbins. (2008). *Nordoff-Robbins music therapy video portrait (part 1)* [Video]. YouTube. https://www.youtube.com/watch?v=_CuAjiU7RBg

Rand, K., & Lahav, A. (2014). Maternal sounds elicit lower heart rate in preterm newborns in the first month of life. *Early Human Development, 90*(10), 679–683.

Reckelhoff, J. (2001). Gender differences in the regulation of blood pressure. *Hypertension, 37*(5), 1199–1208.

The Public Science Lab. (2020). *The Heart Project*. http://robdunnlab.com/projects/beats-per-life/

Turk, E. (2018). *Heartbeat*. Atheneum Books for Young Readers.

Webb, A., Heller, H., Benson, C., & Lahav, A. (2015). Mother's voice and heartbeat sounds elicit auditory plasticity in the human brain before full gestation. *Proceedings of the National Academy of Sciences, 112*(10), 3152-3157.

Krystal L. Demaine

van den Berg, M., Rijnbeek, P., Niemeijer, M., Hoffman, A., van
    Herpen, G., Bots, M., Hillege, H., Swenne, C, Eijgelsheim,
    M., Stricker, B., & Kors, J. (2018). Normal values of corrected
    heart-rate variability in 10-second electrocardiograms for all
    ages. *Frontiers in Physiology*.
    https://doi.org/10.3389/fphys.2018.00424

Chapter 4

Vibrational Energy

Throughout space, all matter is vibrating and all rates of vibration from the lowest musical note to the highest pitch of the chemical rays, hence an atom, or complex of atoms, no matter what its period, must find a vibration with which it is in resonance.
—Thomas Commerford Martin, *The Inventions: Researches and Writings of Nikola Tesla*

Vital-bration

The pulse is a deep, slow vibration that can be felt externally. The vibration can be large or small and both detectable and undetectable, and it is key to all human existence. When we speak the letter *v*, we notice a vibration on our lips. Vibrational words like *violin, vibraphone, vibrato, viable, Valentine, vital, vitamin, vibrant, vibrato,* and *vitality* all conjure meanings related to sound, energy, love, and life, and they tickle our lower lips as we voice them. In 2018, when my son was five years old, I explained the concept of universal vibration to him. I told him that music is vibration, and since vibration creates music and sound energy, music is all around us. Thinking about this idea, he created the word *vital-bration*—a word conveying the understanding that vibration is vital to all existence, to human life, and the universe.

The entire universe is made up of vibrating microscopic particles, each buzzing at a different frequency. It is the chemical makeup of a thing and the frequency of its vibration that makes it what we perceive it to be. My father's favorite scientist Nikola Tesla once said, "If you want to find the secrets of the universe, think in terms of energy, frequency, and vibration" (Nguyen, 2016). Tesla's scientific contributions have still not been fully acknowledged, and many of his inventions have yet to be tested; my dad admired this because a true inventor is not always recognized for his genius. Tesla asserted that vibration comes in many forms, an idea far ahead of his time, which he discovered in his work with electromagnetic engineering. Vibration is active—it produces sound, light, and matter. Science indeed tells us that the rapid frequency of the tiny buzzing particles known as atoms is what gives the illusion of objects being solid. These atomic particles are so minuscule that, if you can picture it, there are more atoms in a grain of sand than there are grains of sand on a small beach. There are 118 kinds of atoms, all presented on the periodic table of elements, which you likely encountered in grade school. About 99 percent of the human body is made up of the following elements: oxygen (65 percent), carbon (18 percent), hydrogen (10 percent), nitrogen (3 percent), calcium (1.5 percent), and phosphorous (1 percent). Each year, the body replaces all of its atoms through drinking, eating, sweating, eliminating, and breathing. Atomic energy becomes stagnant and loses its life in the body without daily replenishment.

The word *vibe* is often used in English to ascribe connection with others. Telling someone "I feel your vibe" or "We are vibing together" lets them know that we sense a symbiotic connection, a sense of empathy or understanding. We may also say that we are on the same frequency or wavelength as another person. As we use our intuition in connecting with others, instinctively sensing another's mood or emotional state, we use these phrases to acknowledge the existence of energy permeating within and between human bodies. Each person resonates at their own vibrational frequency, and attuned individuals may be able to physically feel the vibration or frequency of another. The concept of soul mates perhaps comes down to feeling good because of the way our molecules vibrate together. By surrounding ourselves with positive vibes, which can come from our friendships; our work, home, or school environments; the food we put into our bodies; and even the amount of sleep we get, we can integrate more health into our lives. The key is to increase our exposure to positive vibes.

Frequencies Seen and Felt

Graphic designer and contemplative artist, David Grey has an eye for representing the feeling of frequency and vibration through his digital art. He recalled a time in his life when he was a DJ spinning records in clubs and watching the waves of crowds moving in synchrony to the music. It seemed "as if the music frequency was being represented in a large human sound wave, conducted by the music (D. Grey, personal communication, October 25, 2018).

The field of cymatics gives us a view of what it looks like when a frequency interacts with a material. The term *cymatics*, defined as the visual representation of wave phenomena, was coined by Hans Jenny while researching sound wave visualization using powders and liquids on vibrating plates (Jenny, 1967/2001). Jenny's experiments produced beautiful kaleidoscopic patterns that have been used for book illustrations and covers and framed and hung as artworks in people's homes.

All elements in the universe resonate at their own unique frequency. This includes the human body, each of its organs, the earth, water, and the food we eat. On average, the human body resonates at a frequency between 62 and 78 hertz; however, our bodily frequency can be altered by things such as weather, mood, lighting, foods, and even other people.

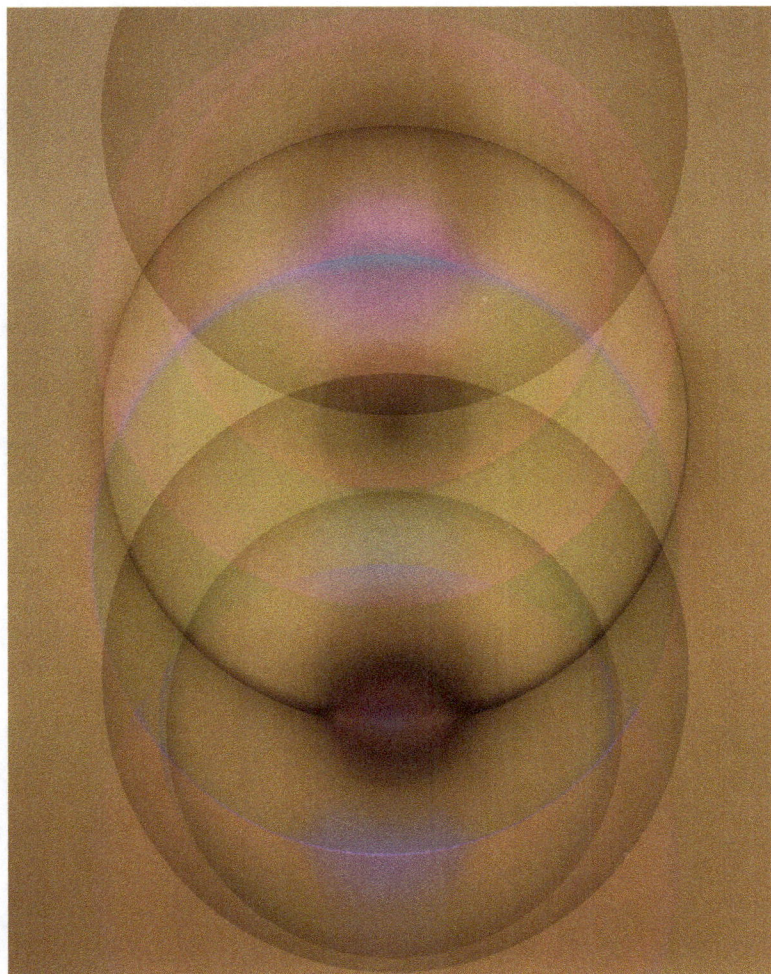

Figure 3. *Untitled Digital Art #1*, 2018. Artist: David Grey.
Reproduced by permission from David Grey.

The vibrations produced by our bodies, the environment, and other animate and inanimate objects can impact the vibrational frequency of the Earth. The Earth has a very low resonant frequency of about 7.83 hertz, which is known as the Schumann resonance. Named for German physicist Winfried Otto Schumann, who discovered the frequency in 1952. The Schumann resonance is sometimes referred to as the Earth's heartbeat. The frequency is produced by the electromagnetic activity within and around the Earth's atmosphere. Dust particles and pollutants sometimes disrupt the electric activity, which explains the relative frequency rate. Most frequency measurements are taken from bodies of water, which is cleaner than the air (English, 2021). As reported by Gibney (2020), there was a noted seismic shift in the Earth's frequency during the COVID-19 lockdowns, which some scientists believe had to do with changes in human activity. Benningfield (2000) suggests that the Schumann resonance is affected not only by environmental changes caused by humans, like deforestation and pollution, but also by human consciousness. The more global stressors are created by humankind, the more the Earth's health will decline.

One element common to the Earth and to humans that is particularly vulnerable to stressors is water. Both the Earth and the human body are composed of about 75 percent water. Just as humans need clean and abundant water to maintain vitality and homeostasis, so does the Earth. The research of Masaru Emoto suggests that not just pollution but vibrational stressors created by humans have an impact on water. In his book *The Hidden Messages in Water*, Emoto (2005) claims that water is impacted by vibrations created by human consciousness. He suggests that since everything is vibrating and therefore is resonating a frequency, everything is creating sound, whether or not it is heard. In his research, Emoto filled Petri dishes with water and exposed the water to various vibrational stimuli, including music, spoken words, typed words, and videos. When he froze the water, the crystallization that resulted produced different patterns. Emoto found that when water was exposed to what was deemed positive stimuli (praying for peace, saying "love," or gentle classical music), the crystals formed symmetrical and aesthetically pleasing shapes. Conversely, when negative stimuli (hateful language, shouting, death metal music) were presented, the crystals resulted in irregular and fragmented forms. Emoto concludes that sound and environment affect not only the human body but the Earth as a whole. Humans, after all, are deeply connected to the earth, as our bodies, and the bodies of plants and other animals are all part of the evolution and history of life. We have seen the Earth's reaction to human violence and aggression against the planet. There has been some skepticism to Emoto's claims, however, we have learned over time that the kinder the human race is to the Earth, the more the Earth will give to the life that exists within it.

Healing Vibes

Known as the "love frequency," 528 hertz has been suggested as the ultimate healing frequency for the human body. A 2019 study conducted by T. Babayi Daylari and colleagues found that 528-hertz sound waves at about a volume of 100 decibels increased testosterone levels and reduced anxiety and oxidation levels in rats. Testosterone affects behavior and memory in mammals in many ways. These findings suggest that this frequency could reduce anxiety and oxidants in human brains as well.

The Lovetuner is a small, shiny, tube-shaped whistle that blows a pitch of 528 hertz. The sound resonates at the pitch note of C, or do, resonating a steady single pitch. It sounds a bit like blowing a single note on the harmonica. The philosophy behind the Lovetuner is grounded in mindfulness approaches. With just a single sound to tune into, one can engage in a simple mindful activity, which promotes calm, increased focus, and wellness. And specifically, when the pitch is 528 hertz, the sound can increase the biofield surrounding the body. Alternative medicine advocate Deepak Chopra suggests that the Lovetuner can be beneficial when played instead of meditation or before and after meditation (Lovetuner 528Hz, 2016).

Whether it is 528 hertz or another frequency, our exposure to other specific vibrations and frequencies can have unique clinical implications. One treatment approach called whole-body vibration is conducted with machines and has been used by athletes since the 1980s. In this approach, a person stands or lies on a machine that has a vibrating platform. The vibration transmits energy to the body, which causes muscle contractions (Sharma et al., 2021). Athletes work with trainers using this approach to help condition their muscles.

A 2018 research investigation conducted by Lage and colleagues in Brazil demonstrated that whole-body vibration helped adults with pulmonary disease. In a study with 26 adults, 13 diagnosed with chronic obstructive pulmonary disease and 13 with normal pulmonary functioning, participants were exposed to six sessions of whole-body vibration at a frequency of 35 Hz (35 pulses per second) for 30 seconds. The research team found that after just one session, the vibration increased the important anti-inflammatory IL-10 among the pulmonary disease group to levels similar to those in the control group.

This finding that low-frequency vibration reduced inflammation among this group suggests vibration as a meaningful treatment method.

In related research, Anggayasti and colleagues (2020) found that low-frequency vibration (20 hertz) was beneficial when applied to cancer cells. The researchers noted that previous research using high-frequency vibration for the same purpose had damaged the surrounding healthy cells. Using a low frequency allowed for just enough vibration to eradicate only the cancerous cells. The researchers found that when cancer cells were vibrated at 20 hertz, the cells died naturally and did not die from vibrational trauma or the disease.

One of the most captivating stories that show the power of vibration to eradicate unhealthy cells was presented by Anthony Holland, a professor of music. In his 2013 TEDx talk at Skidmore College, Holland describes how he dreamed of treating childhood cancer in a way that did not cause children to suffer the effects of toxic drugs (TEDx Talks, 2013). His research found that music can kill more cancer cells than radiation. Toxic treatments such as chemotherapy and radiation end up destroying healthy cells and can cause the person to feel sicker than from cancer alone. By contrast, vibrations at the right frequencies affected only the cancerous cells. Vibration causes heat and potential destruction, and when a living organism is vibrated at a certain frequency, its cells can be dissolved. Holland found a researcher who had created a device that can pinpoint and transmit energy frequencies to single cells. After experimenting with different frequencies, Holland found the magic combination of two frequencies—one low, one 11 times higher—that caused cells to change their shape and begin to disintegrate. They tested this frequency on different types of cancerous cells. They discovered that 100,000 hertz and 300,000 hertz killed 25–42 percent of leukemia cells and slowed the rate of new growth by as much as 65 percent. Up to 60 percent of ovarian cancer cells and pancreatic cancer cells shrank and dissolved. Last, they tested the effects on methicillin-resistant Staphylococcus aureus (MRSA), a type of staph bacteria that is highly resistant to antibiotics and can result in death. They found that the vibrations also killed the MRSA cells. Holland imagines a world where patients with cancer can be treated in hospital cancer solariums whose ceilings are installed with lights that release unique vibrational frequencies. The lights would electrically and nontoxically destroy the cancer cells, allowing patients to receive a noninvasive and comfortable treatment, all through the power of healing vibes.

Energetic Anatomy

Renowned energy healer Cyndi Dale (2009) writes about energetic anatomy, sometimes known as vibrational medicine, which is a field of energy, or aura, that radiates from the body. Dale refers to this energy as the subtle body, consisting of energetic points in the body, like chakras, meridians, nadis, as well as breath. Dale's work as an energy healer is grounded in Eastern healing approaches like Ayurveda and traditional Chinese medicine. As I once described (Demaine, 2015), traditional Chinese medicine is used widely to treat various health conditions and is the sole method used by 40 percent of all health care providers in China. Currently, in the West, the most commonly used approach within traditional Chinese medicine is acupuncture, which involves inserting thin needles into specific meridian points or channels in the human body to tap into the subtle energetic body. Scientific research has found acupuncture to be effective in stress management: it stimulates the nerves, muscles, and connective tissue while also effectively increasing the overall balance and flow of qi in the body (Wild et al., 2020).

The ancient approach to traditional Chinese medicine relies on the five-element theory. The theory identifies relationships between five body organs and elements: lung/metal, liver/wood, kidney/water, heart/fire, and spleen/earth. The five organs also correlate with five colors, sounds, and various other conditions, such as the weather and circadian rhythms. In Chinese music, the scale is composed of five pitches—known in Western music as the pentatonic scale –*penta* is the prefix meaning five. Limited research has supported that each of the five notes resonates with one of the organs (Chen, 2008; de Barros & de Barros, 2007). Working on a fixed-do system (where the syllables are always tied to certain pitches) the corresponding syllabus and pitches with organs are do (C)–heart, re (D)–kidney, mi (E)–pancreas, sol (G)–lung, and la (A)–liver. Sending a tone to its corresponding organ stimulates that organ's energy, and if that organ is lacking health, the vibration promotes a balance of yin and yang and a greater flow of qi (Demaine, 2015). The ancient Indian medical system of Ayurveda which relies on the chakra system, which identifies a correlation between the seven chakra wheels and a diatonic scale–an eight-note, whole tone scale beginning and ending with the same pitch. This diatonic scale is also known as the basic do-re-mi scale in Western music. In Ayurveda the first chakra known as the *root* corresponds to the pitch G, with subsequent chakras ascending the pitch F at the *crown chakra*. In addition, each of the chakras corresponds with a specific color in accordance with the rainbow beginning with the *root chakra* emitting red and ascending to violet at the *crown chakra*. Uniquely, the fourth chakra known as the heart chakra resonates with the pitch "C" which corresponds with the five-element theory in traditional Chinese medicine (Svoboda, 1888).

Balancing or unblocking the chakras, or finding chi within the five organs in the traditional Chinese medicine approach, may involve a number of different interventions based on the food we eat, our environment, moving our bodies, and the sounds that we surround ourselves with.

Food, Sleep, and Good Energy

Good sleep and healthy eating are vital ways to give our bodies good vibrations. Remarkably, both play a role in better overall health and reduced inflammation in the body. Food fuels the body and keeps us healthy; it nourishes our mind, blood, and every organ in our body. Particularly for the heart, eating foods rich in magnesium, like beans, oats, and some nuts, can reduce the risk of cardiovascular disease and diabetic imbalance. As with any diet, it is important to have a balance of foods. Leslie Korn, mental health and integrative medicine specialist, refers to the colorful rainbow of foods as the Brainbow Blueprint (Korn, 2020). The Brainbow is a way of consciously eating to fuel the brain, body, and mind and give the body good energy.

Foods, just like all other things, have a vibrational frequency. Some people believe that eating high-frequency foods brings them good vibrations and a sense of higher consciousness. Food frequency is measured by well-tempered vibrometers and accelerometers. A vibrometer takes the vibrational measurement of an object's surface. An accelerometer uses a piezoelectric sensor to measure an object's energetic voltage. These devices have shown that organic, raw, fresh, and colorful foods resonate at a higher frequency. Foods that are cooked (including no longer living animals), dark, or canned have little to no energetic frequency. Higher-frequency foods have been associated with reduced cancer and disease in the human body.

One simple way to give the body a quick dose of high-energy food is by drinking a glass of water mixed with half of a freshly squeezed lemon or a tablespoon of apple cider vinegar, a natural probiotic, which helps build healthy gut bacteria. Both apple cider vinegar and lemon also increase immunity and reduce inflammation, the cause of many ailments. Lemon, in particular, is rich in vitamin C, fiber, and pectin. Either option can help increase energy, dissolve toxins in the body, and improve digestion. The same effect can be achieved in part by drinking a tea high in antioxidants, such as white, black, and green tea; of these, matcha contains the most antioxidants. I have made it a practice to sip a cup of hot water with a splash of apple cider vinegar first thing every morning and a cup of hot water with the juice of half a lemon each night before bed.

About 75 percent of our immune system function lives in the gut—from cortisol (stress hormone) receptors to the organs that process and distribute food and nutrients. Therefore, managing the bacteria through pre- and probiotics can aid in having a healthy immune system. In addition to raw apple cider vinegar, yogurt, kefir, ginger, and kombucha tea can soothe a nervous or overactive system and promote probiotic gut health. Stress and inflammation can be villainous even to a strong gut and healthy immune system. Stress does not cause ulcers, but when we are stressed, we may turn to aids that can cause a peptic ulcer, such as anti-inflammatory drugs. Such drugs can in turn break down the skin of the gut and stomach lining and therefore impair our overall immunity, causing only more inflammation. This is why natural treatments that reduce stress and inflammation can best promote overall health.

Inflammation can be felt throughout the body, bringing pain and sensitivity to the bones and joints, headaches and pressure to the brain, body bloating, skin conditions, and stress and tension to the heart. Inflammation can be amplified by stress or by eating large amounts of inflammatory foods, such as glutens, sugars, trans fats, and alcohol. The less we are bogged down by inflammation and the more attentive we are to what we eat, the better our vibrational frequencies.

When it comes to sleep, our patterns and cycles of rest can affect metabolism, alertness, health, wellness, and inflammatory response. Sleep problems, which prevent us from getting the much-needed and recommended eight hours of sleep, can also contribute to increased inflammation and low immunity. Good sleep hygiene practices such as going to bed around the same time each night, not watching television or looking at a smartphone before bed, and sleeping in a space that is quiet and has fresh, cool air can all help us to get better-quality sleep. It is also important to stop eating a few hours before bed to allow the body time to digest. Digestion is a method of fuel burning that can actually keep us awake at night. Good sleep helps us to feel energized and more conscious in our day-to-day tasks.

Sometimes, when we get good sleep, we can function and feel refreshed on less of it. According to anthropologist A. Roger Ekirch (2006), during preindustrial times, people never slept straight through the night. Rather than a single eight-hour stretch, our sleeping schedule had two sleep shifts. According to Ekirch, people fell asleep at dusk, were active in the middle of the night, and then slept more. During the overnight awake time, people would do things like have sex, converse with their partners, think about their dreams, and do work, such as preparing food, cleaning, or reading. The two-sleep cycle faded away during the late 1700s. Today, if we cannot sleep the full eight hours at night, we can still get the amount of sleep we need through naps and other forms of rest, such as meditation and yoga. Yoga nidra, a form of meditation whose name is translated as "sleep yoga," is one effective technique (Saraswati, 1976).

Our internal body clock, our circadian rhythm, tracks our tasks of living, sleeping, and eating. This internal rhythm is governed by nature, through the tides, the winds, the sun, our environment, and the foods we eat. Further, humans create a flow together with nature (Demaine, 2015). The closer we can get to nature by eating natural foods, relying on the sun to guide our sleep, spending time in more peaceful and natural environments, and walking about two miles a day, we will become more in tune with the rhythm of our heart, and feel more healthful and energetic.

Sympathetic Resonance

When it comes to our rhythms, humans have a natural way of syncing up or tuning into one another. We exhibit synchrony when we begin to walk at the same tempo as the person walking next to us or when we play in a drum circle and adjust our tempos to play together. One of the earliest reports of this phenomenon was in 1665 by Dutch physicist Christiaan Huygens, inventor of the pendulum clock. He noticed that when clocks were hung next to one another on a wall, pendulums that began to swing at different times would eventually (about 30 minutes later) begin to move in synchrony. Huygens called his discovery an "odd sympathy" (Ramirez et al., 2016, p. np)—which we now call entrainment. This natural entrainment of frequencies occurs in nature through biological systems and in our movements. Huygens surmised that the air molecules sent vibrations of the same frequency to each pendulum. He noticed, however, that the same effect did not result when the clocks were laid flat on a table and hypothesized that when the clocks were not hung on a wall, there was an interruption of the vibrational frequency.

A neurologic perspective on synchronicity and its role in empathy has been highlighted by the proposed mirror neuron system in humans, which Indian American neuroscientist V. S. Ramachandran (2000) suggested would do for neuroscience what DNA did for biology.

This group of neurons was first discovered in the 1990s by a research group in Parma, Italy, in the brain of a macaque monkey. The researchers embedded a single-cell measurement device in the monkey's brain to assess when neurons were firing in coordination with another task. By chance, the investigator noticed that when the monkey simply saw or heard the investigator eating a peanut, the same neurons fired in the monkey's brain. This was the case whether the researcher ate a peanut, pantomimed eating a peanut, and only made the crunch sound (di Pellegrino et al., 1992). A similar mirror neuron system exists in humans. The research on mirror neurons tells us that our brain is activated to sense what other people are doing, even if we do not do it ourselves.

Mirror neurons may also help explain limitations in language and communication abilities among nonverbal children with autism (Wan et al., 2010). Mirror neurons play a vital role in expressive and receptive speech and language, not only for the development of imitation of language (a pillar of language learning) but also for understanding the meaning of what someone is communicating. Therefore, disruption of mirror neurons can explain the lack of empathetic understanding among this population. In 2006, an issue of *Scientific American* featured a cover of a child sitting on a broken mirror with the headline "Broken Mirrors: A Theory of Autism." Within that issue, Ramachandran and Oberman (2006) said, "The mirror neuron theory gives a strong neurologic perspective on the functional working of brain regions and neural connections that help promote empathy and understanding."

Synchronicity

Sometimes we get the feeling within our bodies that something is going to happen; some call this feeling intuition or empathetic tuning. The energy that we receive, whether psychically or intuitively, is a signal that activates our central nervous system. In 2019, on a trip to San Francisco, I visited Alcatraz, the former federal prison located on its own island in San Francisco Bay. Alcatraz ceased operations in the 1960s, and today, visitors can take a boat from the port to the island and do a self-guided tour. In the prison, tourists are allowed to step into a few of the small isolation rooms. When I walked into one of those small cells, I felt as if all of the energy was completely sucked from my body; I felt depleted and wasted and almost stuck. My nervous system was telling me to leave, yet the overwhelming feeling of that prison cell seemed to have taken ahold of me. The room felt like a giant magnet extracting my life force. I wondered if it was the type of metal used in the room that was causing my reaction or if it was the physical energy in that space, which held the memories and pain of the prisoners once held there, that was making made me feel so sick. Whatever it was, I walked out of that jail cell feeling negative vibes so strong that I literally needed to shake them from my body.

Human nervous systems respond to each other, and when people are physically and emotionally close, they show physiological synchronicity. A study conducted at the University of California, Davis, found that couples in romantic relationships automatically sync their heart rates and respiration (Helm et al., 2012). This was found by studying 32 heterosexual couples who sat in a quiet room a few feet away from each other without talking or touching. The same physiological matching occurred when the couples were asked to nonverbally imitate each other's posture and movements. When researchers mixed the couples with other partners, their heart rates did not sync up. In addition, they noticed that a woman's heart rate synchronized faster with a man's than a man's did a woman's. The researchers interpreted this result as showing a greater sense of empathy among women. It is already known that we can identify emotions in our partners, but this study further shows that shared physiological experience is at the heart of romantic partnerships.

According to the HeartMath Institute (McCraty, 2003), an organization that has identified the electromagnetic field of the heart, this organ produces the strongest rhythmic electromagnetic field of any organ in the human body. Its electromagnetic field is 60 times greater than that of the brain and can be detected up to three feet away from the body. It is so powerful that it can alter the DNA of a baby inside a mother's womb. Furthermore, HeartMath researchers have discovered that emotional states are encoded in the heart, which then communicates emotions to the external environment. These emotions were measured as energy frequencies from the body using electrocardiogram data. Finally, researchers have also found that the heart signals of one person can affect another person's brain waves, resulting in heart-brain synchronicity between two people.

The good vibrations arising from being around people whom we have energetic sympathy with can actually increase dopamine levels in the brain and serotonin levels in the gut. We see this with mothers and their babies, who both produce the widely known "love hormone," oxytocin when they are in contact. The pleasure we receive from these neurochemicals actually makes us more attracted to those people and, in some cases, addicted to those people. Social resonance (which influences our ability to form successful relationships) can engage the opioid receptors, creating a sense of pleasure and a desire for more of the same experience. The same type of reaction occurs in opioid drug users (Merrer et al., 2009). But it is important to note that these chemicals can be accessed through natural, healthy frequencies in the body. We all can pick up good vibes, tune into the authentic frequencies of others, and generate healthy energetic consciousness in our lives, as long as we are conscious energetic beings.

The Capacity for Empathy

We begin to develop our sense of empathy during infancy. In the 1970s, Andrew N. Meltzoff and M. Keith Moore (1977) were the first to research how newborn babies imitate others. They found that at just two weeks old, babies can mimic facial expressions, which are the precursors to social development and emotional understanding. Humans naturally tend to mimic another person's posture and movements as an unconscious signal of empathy. The natural human inclination to move like those we are with is called the chameleon effect (Chartrand & Bargh, 1999). It is this unconscious imitation of behaviors that allows us to engage socially with people who are unlike us.

Empathy is the capacity to sense another person's emotions and to be a part of their experience because we have experienced it in our own lives. It is the pathway to compassion. Science journalist Maia Szalavitz and psychiatrist Bruce D. Perry (2010) note in their book *Born for Love* that "empathy is deeply rooted in our biology" and that "even bacteria can sense the presence of other species" (p. 13). Humans are naturally capable of empathy. Sometimes, however, we can be so empathetic that we can absorb the energy of others and carry it as our own. Empathic boundaries and awareness of how much we can carry are therefore important so that we do not take on too much of someone else's pain.

About three months before my father died, his refrain became "I'm just not feeling well." About a year before that, he fell into a challenging sleeping pattern. He was not able to sleep until late and so woke up at 1 p.m. every day and was back in bed by 4 p.m. He had no desire to go out and see his friends. He became fatigued, and for a year-and-a-half or so prior to all of this, his hands developed a perpetual Parkinson's-like tremor, which he struggled to hide. Even his handwriting became less legible –smaller and more ragged. Day after day, he lay in his bed, he slept, he ignored people, he was angry, he was depressed; his mood had changed and he was just not himself. After Dad died, Mom would not go into the bedroom where she had once slept with Dad. She lived entirely in the TV room. It was probably easier to cope, imagining that Dad was still sleeping and resting in bed and that living in the TV room would mean he would not be interrupted. During this time, my mom told us that a couple of weeks before Dad's death his insomnia intensified, and he would be up for much of the night, many times he would call my mother into the bedroom confused and hallucinating, pointing out things in the room that weren't even there. When he eventually fell asleep, he would thrash around in his sleep and my mother would retreat to the couch to get some sleep herself. When my sisters and were alerted to Dad's behavior change we thought it was a result of his lack of sleep and confusion related to insomnia. In November 2018, I wrote in my journal:

> *I'm sitting at the kitchen counter in my apartment with a cup of tea next to me. Turmeric tea with ginger —this will help reduce the inflammation in my joints and pressure in my hips and ankles; maybe I need to lose weight, and maybe it's just my metabolism slowing down as I am getting older. I have taken too many anti-inflammatory drugs and sinus medications to help the stress in my body that has extended from my joints to my eyes, to my brain. All of this family court stuff [with my son's father] is taking an awful toll on me. My daily sinus headaches are only slightly relieved when I put pressure above my eyes, which I think might be stimulating my vagus nerve. I am not doing as much yoga as I used to, and not playing as much music. And when I rub my eyes, which I do often now because I just feel exhausted, my vision has become distorted and my eye doctor has said the eye rubbing has caused an onset of keratoconus, a thinning of the cornea, resulting in my now blurred vision–just like dad. After four visits to the optometrist over the course of two months and a follow-up with my primary care doctor, the advice I got was to get more sleep, meditate more, and keep my eyes out of the sun and away from the computer.*

In December 2018, with Dad's symptoms increasing and everything folding into the center, I began to recognize that my physical pain and tension were highly synchronized to the conditions my father was experiencing. On my son's fifth birthday, December 16, 2018, just two weeks before Dad died, we had a small family birthday party at my parent's apartment. My dad was resting in his room and only came out briefly while we were eating quiche and salad at the kitchen table. Mom said that Dad was not eating. The doctors put him on the very bland BRAT (bananas, rice, apple sauce, toast) diet. That day, I felt deep sadness for my father. At one moment in front of my family, while Dad was tucked away in his bed, I put my hand on his bedroom door and said out loud, *"Dad is dying."* I had the intuitive feeling that he was losing his life. I felt a complete loss of emotion and engagement in my body and mind as I touched his bedroom door with him inside. It was almost like being back at Alcatraz in the prison cell. My body felt heavy and hollow.

Energetic Consciousness

Nikola Tesla had a sense that there is more to energy than just particles, that there is a frequency that each particle contains that allows for interexchange of information and that human conscious awareness could increase the resonant frequency of things. Tesla came to these ideas through his practice of Kundalini yoga and was intrigued by how the practice of mindfulness raised his level of consciousness (Kreutzer, n.d.). *Kundalini* is a term that describes energy at rest. A practice of Kundalini awakening through meditation has been said to increase conscious awareness and help lead to the path of enlightenment, which involves a physical shift in the nervous system and spine (Lockley, 2019). This supposed shift of consciousness is said to change a person's vibrational frequency.

In his TEDx talk, sports and marketing executive David Meltzer (TEDx Talks, 2019) says that we are all able to live an authentic life by finding our unique frequency. He describes learning this lesson while on a flight and sitting next to a woman from India named Sangeeta Sahi. She told him that he was so full of light, but he was blocking it. Busy with his work, he at first dismissed her statement. The woman then asked if he meditated, and he said that he did not have time for this. She said that she could teach him to meditate in order to vibrate faster. She explained that we can only be aware of things that vibrate slower than we do, and because truth vibrates fastest of all, we must vibrate even faster and become aware of our frequency. That awareness allows us to be more conscious. If we know our frequency, Meltzer explains, we achieve calm in knowing what is true within us, and there is no desire to impress others. Our frequency may not be a numerical expression of vibration but more our mood or behavior. Once we find our frequency, the energy that feels good to us, our baseline, our evenness, then we must stick to it to radiate our authentic self. In essence, we don't need to invent who we are we just need to remove all of the things that shroud our true self, our true heart.

As mentioned earlier, the energy that our bodies encounter on a day-to-day basis comes from all over the world, through the food we eat, the water we drink, the air we breathe, and the people and places we surround ourselves with. Energetic protons, neutrons, and electrons are the tiny foundations within every atom of all elements. From the beginning of life to death, the energy that inhabits the human body forms skin, blood, connection to others, and consciousness. It is consciousness that keeps humans rooted in the river of life as we know it and also gives us many questions about the meaning of life and the purpose of human existence. When we die, the conscious awareness once housed in our bodies and brains goes quite possibly, like all energy does, simply back into the universe of particles. However, in a way, consciousness is ethereal, an idea that continues to puzzle humankind. Science has indicated that atoms do not disappear—they continue to exist as part of the fabric of the universe.

Companion Listening #4

"Swallow" by The Wailin' Jennys (2006)

Creative Exercise #4: Heart Card

For this exercise, you will be creating a visual representation of your heart using any art materials that are accessible to you. Art materials can come from nature, such as sand, stone, or tree twigs; or you can use more traditional art supplies, such as paint, paper, or drawing or collage materials. Once you have gathered your materials, sit for a moment and tune into the heart as you did in the previous exercises. Using intuition and without engaging the thinking brain, begin to offer an aesthetic response to your heart by creating a visual representation using the materials. The representation can be abstract or representational, and it can include symbols, images, lines, shapes, or colors. The intuitive and spontaneous response to the heart is key. Try not to agonize over what you are creating or to overthink its meaning. The key is to create a visual representation of how you see your heart. Consider the symbols and forms that are in your heart, what surrounds your heart, and what your heart radiates.

Once you have finished creating your heart card, first sit with it in front of you. Second, begin to record, either mentally or on paper, your objective observations; simply record what you see. For example, *I see the color pink on the edges, I see a symbol in the center,* or *I see jagged lines running to the edges.* Next, quickly write down your subjective observations; record your inferences, making meaning from the symbols and lines. For example, *The jagged lines running to the edges are my heart pouring out,* or *The color green means that I am seeking something specific in my life.*

Next, begin to write freely and fluidly about what you created. Begin to create some written meaning-making in your art. Write freely for five or ten minutes. Once you are done, read what you have written and underline or circle a single phrase or more that strikes you aesthetically, giving you a tingling or moving feeling.

Finally, you will create a mantra based on your selected phrase (or phrases). This mantra is a healing, nurturing message to the heart. Using the phrase from your writing or creating a new phrase, add it to the blank space in the following sentence: *My heart is* ____. Now add the wishes for your heart: *My heart wish is* ____. State these phrases to yourself three times, with your hand over your heart to bring the mindful conscious awareness in the positive mantra to your heart center.

References

Anggayasti, W. L., Imashiro, C., Kuribara, T., Totani, K., & Takemura, K. (2020). Low-frequency mechanical vibration induces apoptosis of A431 epidermoid carcinoma cells. *Engineering in Life Sciences, 20*(7), 232–238. https://doi.org/10.1002/elsc.201900154

Babayi Daylari, T., Riazi, G. H., Pooyan, Sh., Fathi, E., & Katouli, F. H. (2019). Influence of various intensities of 528 hertz sound-wave in production of testosterone in rat's brain and analysis of behavioral changes. *Gene Genomics, 41*(2), 201–211.

Benningfield, D. (2020, May 20), Studying Earth's double electrical heartbeat. *Eos, 101.* https://doi.org/10.1029/2020EO143519

Chartrand, T. L., & Bargh, J. A. (1999). The chameleon effect: The perception-behavior link and social interaction. *Journal of Personality and Social Psychology, 76*(6), 893-910.

Chen, Z. (2008). Chinese music's five elements, five tones. *The Epoch times.* http://en.epochtimes.com/n2/china/chinese-music-five-elements-5137.html

Dale, C. (2009). *The subtle body: An encyclopedia of your energetic anatomy.* Sounds True.

de Barros, F.C., & de Barros, S. E. (2007). The fundamental frequency of voice and its correlations with the five sounds of traditional Chinese medicine. *Acupuncture & Electro-Therapeutics Research International Journal, 32*, 211-221.

Demaine, K. (2015). Musical roots for healing: The five-tone system in traditional Chinese medicine. In S. L. Brooke (Ed.), *Therapists creating a cultural tapestry: Using the creative therapies across cultures* (pp. 154–169). Charles C. Thomas.

di Pellegrino, G., Fadiga, L., Fogassi, L., Gallese, V., & Rizzolatti, G. (1992). Understanding motor events: A neurophysiological study. *Experimental Brain Research, 91*, 176-180.

Ekirch, A. R. (2006). *At day's close: Night in times past.* W. W. Norton.

Emoto, M. (2005). *The hidden messages in water.* Atria Books.

English, T. (2021, January 2). *Schumann resonance: Does Earth's 7.83 Hz "heartbeat" influence our behavior?* Interesting Engineering. https://interestingengineering.com/what-is-the-schumann-resonance

Gibney, E. (2020, March 31). *Coronavirus lockdowns have changed the way the Earth moves.* Nature. https://www.nature.com/articles/d41586-020-00965-x

Helm, J., Sbarra, D., & Ferrer, E. (2012). Assessing cross-partner associations in psychological responses via coupled oscillator

models. *Emotion 12*(4), 748–862.
https://doi.org//10.1037/a0025036

Horowitz, L. (2019, May). Quantum conversation with Len
Horowitz—528 Love Frequency.
https://poddtoppen.se/podcast/1195706930/quantum-
conversations/quantum-conversation-with-dr-len-horowitz-
528-love-frequency

Jenny, H. (2001). *Cymatic* (3rd ed.). MACROmedia. (Original work
published 1967)

Korn, L. (2020, July 15). The brainbrow blueprint for mental health.
Spirituality and Health.
https://www.spiritualityhealth.com/articles/2020/04/13/the
-brainbow-blueprint-for-mental-health

Meltzoff, A. N., & Moore, M. K. (1977). Imitation of facial and
manual gestures by human neonates. *Science*, 198, 75–78.

Kreutzer, V. (n.d.). *Nikola Tesla*. Institute for Consciousness Research.
https://www.icrcanada.org/research/literaryresearch/tesla

Lage, V., Lacerda, A. C., Neves, C., Chaves, M. Soares, A., Lima, L.,
Martins, J., Matos, M., Viera, E., Teixeira, A., Leite, H.,
Oliveira, V., & Mendonca, V. (2018). Acute effects of whole-
body vibration on inflammatory markers in people with
chronic obstructive pulmonary disease: A pilot study.
Rehabilitation Research and Practice, 5480214.
https://doi.org//10.1155/2018/5480214

Lockley, M. (2019). Kundalini awakening, kundalini awareness. *Journal
of the Study of Religious Experience*, 5(1). https://rerc-
journal.tsd.ac.uk/index.php/religiousexp/article/view/59

Lovetuner 528hz. (2016, March 10). *Deepak Chopra introduces the
Lovetuner* [Video]. YouTube.
https://www.youtube.com/watch?v=AuYN4S1DywE&t=3s

Martin, T. C. (1894). *The inventions: Researches and writings of Nikola Tesla.*
Harvard University.

McCraty, R. (2003). *The energetic heart.* Institute of HeartMath.

Merrer, J., Becker, J., Befort, K., & Kieffer, B. (2009). Reward
processing by the opioid system in the brain. *Physiological
Review*, 89(4), 1279–1412.

Nguyen, T. (2016). *History of humans* (Is there a God? Book 3).
EnCognitive.com

Ramachandran, V. S. (2000). Mirror neurons and imitation learning as
the driving force behind the Great Leap Forward in human
evolution. *Edge*, 69.

https://www.edge.org/conversation/vilayanur_ramachandra
n-mirror-neurons-and-imitation-learning-as-the-driving-force

Ramachandran, V. S., & Oberman, L. M. (2006, November). Broken mirrors: A theory of autism. *Scientific American, 295*(5). https://www.scientificamerican.com/article/broken-mirrors-a-theory-of-autism/

Ramirez, J., Olvera, L., Nijmeijer, H., & Alvarez, J. (2016). The sympathy of two pendulum clocks: Beyond Huygen's observations. *Scientific Reports, 6* (23580). https://www.nature.com/articles/srep23580

Saraswati, S. S. (1976). *Yoga nidra.* Yoga Publications Trust / Munger.

Sharma, S., Saifi, S., Arora, N. K. R., & Sharma, S. (2021). Whole body vibration for athletes: An evidence informed review. *Journal of Clinical and Diagnostic Research, 15*(5), 6–10.

Svoboda, R. (1998). *Pratriki: Your ayurvedic constitution.* Lotus Press.

Szalavitz, M., & Perry, B. D. (2010). *Born for love: Why empathy is essential—and endangered.* HarperCollins.

TEDx Talks. (2013, December 22). *Shattering cancer with resonant frequencies: Anthony Holland at TEDxSkidmoreCollege* [Video]. YouTube. https://youtu.be/1w0_kazbb_U

TEDx Talks. (2019, June 20). *Find your frequency | David Meltzer | TEDxDesignTechHighSchool* [Video]. YouTube. https://www.youtube.com/watch?v=qWkLtHxV63Y

Wan, C., Demaine, K., Zipse, L., Norton, A., & Schlaug, G. (2010). From music making to speaking: Engaging the mirror neuron system in autism. *Brain Research Bulletin, 82,* 161–168.

Wild, B., Brenner, J., Joos, S., Samstag, Y., Buckert, M., & Valentini, J. (2020). Acupuncture in persons with an increased stress level-Results from a randomized-controlled pilot trial. *PLoS One, 15*(7): e0236004. doi: 10.1371/journal.pone.0236004. PMID: 32701

Chapter 5

Sound Energy

The medicine of the future will be music and sound.
—Edgar Cayce

Play for love, my glorious musician, keep playing your inspiring tunes, do not stop.
You are my only friend, the solace of my soul, do not leave now that my heart has
fallen in love feeling so tender and open to pain. Unlike man's sorrows that taste
bitter Love's pain is sweet, do not avoid it for if it leaves you even for a moment
your heart will turn into a tomb and you into a mourner. Embrace the pain of
Love, let it be your comfort and the sorrows of the night will end.
—Rumi

Mother Nature's Powerful Resonators

Sounds have an energy that we can feel, hear, and connect to through
our emotions. In early summer on the North Shore of Massachusetts,
where I live, a deep resonating sound can be heard buzzing from the
trees. This is the sound of the June bug. These insects emerge from the
soil at the end of the spring, almost out of nowhere, after hibernating in
latency. Walking out on the front porch on the morning of July 14, 2019,
my son and I found a June bug lying on its back. This is the way June
bugs and many other bugs die, assuming a familiar position, on the back
with legs crossed and pointed up to the sky. That morning, my son and
I heard a quote on the radio—"You only die once. Make sure you do it
right." This is true, just as we are also born only once —and we have to
do what it takes to make our lives fulfilling. Sometimes we can decide
what we want our death to be like—who will be present, what will be
said, and where it will all take place. Other times we do not have the
choice, and we have to accept the hand of cards that we have been dealt.
My son and I wanted this June bug to feel comforted in death, so we
decided how its last moments would be. We surrounded the dying
creature with flowers, burning incense, and my father's yahrzeit candle,
and we played sacred music. We sat and observed the insect. In the last
few moments before "June" died, it became deeply active, stretching its
legs and spreading its wings vigorously, then finally beginning to turn
its body over for one last walkabout. My son thought that maybe June

was coming back for another round of life. At that moment, I had a flashback to my music therapy work in hospice with a patient dying of metastatic breast cancer, whose body began to thrash, stretch, and show signs of delusion and confusion just before her last moment of life. I recalled at that moment how this patient died alone in her room. Her husband refused to come to the hospice to say goodbye as he wanted to remember her living at home rather than imprint in his mind an image of her in a clinical setting. In June's last moments, my son and I heard a call in the air, the buzzing sound of June bugs once again. Despite the sound of an airplane overhead, the blue jays cawing, the sacred chant music playing from my phone, and the warm summer breeze rustling through the leaves on the trees, the June bugs resounded more powerfully and magically, encompassing the entire soundscape.

The June bug, or June beetle, is part of the scarab family. In ancient Egyptian mythology, the scarab beetle was a spiritual symbol of immortality and transformation. Carl Jung, the founder of analytic psychology, has a famous story of the golden scarab beetle, which brought the study of synchronicity in the universe to the attention of psychological researchers (Beitman, 2020). In his analytic work, Jung had a therapy session with an affluent woman who dreamed she was given a golden scarab beetle. Just as she was telling Jung the dream, he leaned back in his chair and heard a light tapping on the window pane behind him. He opened the window, reached his hand out, and to his surprise, a scarab beetle flew right into his palm. Jung handed the woman the beetle as a symbol of the relationship between the dream world and the wakeful conscious present.

When we are open to the frequencies that surround us—the signals, sounds, and energies in whatever form the energy presents—there is an opportunity for connections with and realizations of the world around us. Whether it is a synchronous experience or the universe telling us to listen, the key is being open to receiving energy. We have receptors throughout our body that can receive electrical impulses and sensory information. Music is electric via its impulses and wave forms. These impulses sent to the ears can be mostly pleasing, depending on an individual's auditory perceptual processing. While the hissing of the June bug may not be pleasant to hear, its sound is resonant and, in a way, stimulates the nervous system, just as music does, perhaps conjuring unique thoughts, memories, feelings, and emotions.

The Physics of Sound
In *The Listening Book*, composer and music teacher W. A. Mathieu (1991) presents listening scenarios, written as short essays, to explore the

interplay of music and sound with everyday life. From the wind whipping in the trees to the waves crashing on the beach, sound is everywhere, and if we listen deeply, we can begin to notice differences in pitch and underlying rhythm. Just as Milford Graves was able to identify melodies and pitches by listening to heartbeats, we can begin to tune in to the melodies and sounds in all of nature and our environment—the ostinato pattern of birds tweeting, the rhythms of children playing in the street, and the beat of hammers nailing a roof onto a house. Like David Grey illustrates below in a single pulse (of sound) that resonates into concentric circles interacting with one another. Just by listening, we can begin to notice new sound qualities and intermingle our sounds to create music throughout the day.

Acoustics is a musical term dealing with the study of the physics of sound. Acoustics is grounded in how sound is produced, transmitted, and perceived by the human auditory system; and technically speaking, acoustics deals with the ultra-tiny wave particles that create sound. In English, the term *acoustic* is used to describe musical instruments like guitars, pianos, winds, and horns when they are heard without amplification. However, acoustics deals with the production of all kinds of sound, not just a specific group of musical instruments.

The field of acoustics also includes the concepts of volume, pitch, and frequency. Volume has to do with how loud or soft something sounds, and it is measured in the unit of decibels. Humans can typically hear sounds between 10 and 140 decibels. However, a continuous sound of 75 decibels (a sustained vacuum cleaner or machinery sounds) or higher can over time cause permanent hearing damage, and 120 decibels (rock concerts or car races) or higher can cause immediate hearing damage. The volume or intensity of sound is measured by something known as amplitude. Amplitude has to do with the actual size of the sound wave. If you can imagine sound waves oscillating through the air, they would look like waves grooving along, just like waves in the ocean. Larger amplitude, or bigger waves, are produced when a greater force is applied to the original sound being created. Imagine being the only person sitting in the very last row of a large concert hall. Then suddenly, with full force, a tuba player on the stage blows the loudest, most robust, single, low bass pitch. The force of the blow creates a sound wave that is so big that its sound travels back to your seat in the hall, and your ears are still able to perceive its volume. Because of the force (amplitude), or big push, of the waves, the pitch sustains its motion through the air to be heard by you.

Figure 4. *Untitled Digital Art #2*, 2018. Artist: David Grey.
Reproduced by permission from David Grey.

Psychoacoustics

Psychoacoustics is a scientific field that examines the quality of sound perception in humans. When we talk about sound, this can include musical sounds, nonmusical sounds, or other noise. Musical sounds are usually considered pleasing to the ear, with symmetrical sound waves, an ongoing pattern, and deliberate pitches. As discussed earlier, Masaru

Emoto found that water crystallized in a symmetrical pattern when exposed to gentle classical music. Humans also respond favorably to such pleasing sounds. We find the voices of some people to be soothing. Voices that are more pleasing to our ears tend to have a fuller, balanced melodic tone. Italian, French, Russian, and Spanish are among the most melodic and musical languages (Kogan & Reiterer, 2021). Spoken Chinese—which has eight dialects, including Mandarin and Cantonese—relies upon slight changes in tone to produce new words (Bolotnikov, n.d.).

> With consideration to tonal languages, a sound in English, for example, "ma" can be spoken or intoned in four different ways in Chinese languages, each with a different meaning. Thus, the tonal language speaker has a natural sense of tone shape and sound quality. Researchers have found that 60% of Chinese speakers demonstrate the criteria for absolute pitch. (Demaine, 2015, p. 163)

The simplest and most fundamental sound is produced by the sine wave. The sine wave electrically creates a clean and unwavering tone, and it is often used in research as it is a pure tone that does not produce any additional harmonics. Typically, when we hear a single pitch, our ears can determine additional overtones from that one sound—this is not the case with the pure sine wave tone. The Emergency Alert System, uses a two-tone sine wave, at 853 hertz and 960 hertz simultaneously, as its National Alert System sound. Most people living in the United States who have owned a television at least since the 1990s will be familiar with the infamously loud emergency broadcast tones, accompanied by an announcement that alerts its listeners, "This is only a test."

The Mechanics of Hearing Sound

While the human body can perceive the vibration produced by sound on the skin, the hearing of sound typically begins with the ear. Sound waves travel first down the interior of the ear's air canal (the part that we clean with a cotton swab) until they reach the tympanic membrane, also known as the eardrum. The eardrum is built of a thin flap of skin that is stretched tight, just like a drum, which begins to vibrate when it encounters sound waves. The eardrum is the first area that separates the outer ear from the middle part of the ear.

The eardrum's function can be compared to the large drum known as the timpani, or kettledrum, that is performed at the back of an orchestra. This drum is one of the biggest of the percussion family, with a large drumhead stretched over a huge copper metal bowl. The timpani is the powerhouse of the orchestra: with its deep, rumbling tones and dynamic range, it leads its partner instruments as it supports the rhythm, melody, and harmony. Like the timpani, the eardrum is responsible for sending sound vibrations throughout the inner part of the ear. As the eardrum begins to vibrate, the three tiniest bones in the human body, the anvil, the hammer, and the stirrup, known collectively as the auditory ossicles, begin their vibrational performance. The ossicles' vibration sends sound waves onto the cochlea, a snail-shaped mechanism in the brain, and its semicircular canals. The canals are fixed together and appear like three pieces of elbow-shaped pasta rising above the cochlea. The canals and the cochlea are filled with fluid. As the fluid moves with sound vibrations, the tiny hairs in the cochlea are set in motion, which in turn sends electrical impulses to the neurotransmitters that travel to the auditory nerves in the brain. Attached to the tiny hair cells are even tinier crystals, sometimes referred to as ear stones. The stones help give our vestibular system a sense of balance and organization. At times, these crystals can become loose and fall off, displacing the fluid levels and triggering a sensation of dizziness or vertigo. Generally speaking, movements such as standing up and moving around cause the tiny hairs in the cochlea to move but do not cause the crystals to fall off. Engaging this vestibular system is important to help keep our bodies grounded and balanced. To better engage our sensory system, children and adults alike should walk on balance beams, bounce on pogo sticks, ride bikes, walk through the woods over bumpy roots, and practice balance poses in yoga!

Prana and the Flute

The breath is one of the most powerful tools the human body has to control its vibrational energy. Deep and mindful breathing reduces stress and elicits relaxation, as exemplified in yoga and meditation practices (Harvard Health Publishing, 2020). When we become anxious or stressed, the heart and mind can run wild, engaging the sympathetic nervous system. It is the breath that has the power to rein in these overenthusiastic organs and tap into our parasympathetic nervous system. Thus, the act of breathing helps to recalibrate the body and organizes the central nervous system.

While breath can soothe the heart and tune into the central nervous system, it is also the most important component of human life. The breath delivers the body's life force in the form of oxygen. If we cannot breathe, we are not able to give our cells life. Humans can go about three days without water and even more days without food—but unless we are Olympic swimmers, most humans can live only a couple of minutes without air.

When it comes to breath work in my personal and clinical practice, I have called upon singing, breathing techniques, and flute playing to engage pranayama, a yogic practice of controlling the breath. In Sanskrit, *prana* means breath or life energy, and *yama* means restraint or control. Prana in yoga is essential to vitality and is engaged through activities similar to what I have adopted in my practice—breathing exercises, singing, chanting, and playing flutes and other wind instruments. There is some evidence that musicians who play wind instruments have stronger autonomic regulation than nonmusicians (Czycyk, et al., 2020). Autonomic regulation involves nervous system processes that function automatically, such as breathing, heart rate, and blood pressure. If we have better breath control, we have a greater opportunity to regulate the nervous system.

Growing up with a musician as a parent meant that music was a part of my everyday environment. When I was eight years old, my father asked me what musical instrument I wanted to learn. Without hesitation, I stated, "The flute." There was something magical to me about the flute; its silver color, spritely intonation, and small size attracted me. Soon after this conversation with my father, I started with private flute lessons, studying classical and baroque music. When I was a teenager and listening to a lot of jazz, my father invited me to play flute with his jazz buddies. At Berklee College of Music, my flute repertoire expanded to blues, Latin, and klezmer music. After college, before starting my private practice, I briefly played flute on tour with a funky bluegrass band. The flute has been my principal instrument and one that I always use in my music therapy practice.

As I integrated flute work into my music therapy practice, I transitioned from the silver flute and incorporated handmade wooden flutes along with other smaller flutes like the ocarina, kazoo, slide whistle, and recorder. My favorite flute is the Native American drone flute, which involves two attached flutes. One flute is a typical fingered wooden flute; the other has a similar construction but plays only a single harmonized tone. With the sound of the drone flute, one can tune into the separate drone sound or enjoy an all-encompassing soundscape that combines melody and harmony.

I have used the flute with clients across the entire life span and from diverse populations—including adults and children in hospice, teens with autism, adults with neurologic impairment, psychiatric patients, and the most medically fragile children. I begin by describing the nature of the flute—what it is made of, the sound it creates—and how it has been used for tens of thousands of years. Archaeologists have found ancient Neanderthal flutes made out of animal bone. The oldest flute was found in Slovenia in 1995 and was estimated to be 45,000 years old (Turk, 1997). In my practice, depending on the population, I sometimes invite the person to play the flute to their abilities. Sometimes the flute is used for listening and relaxation, as a cue for breathing, or as stimulation for the parasympathetic nervous system's relaxation response. One boy with autism who spoke with very staccato vocal sounds was challenged to deepen his breath support by playing the flute. I started bringing slide whistles to his music therapy session to see if he could create sounds naturally and learn to expand those sounds with breath. Eventually, he was able to blow the slide whistle completely. His increased breath support and strength in turn helped to develop his speech fluency and to calm his body (Demaine, 2009).

The flute has also been beneficial in enhancing the most minute motor faculties. One child with very limited movement placed their fingers over mine as I played the silver flute. As the sounds changed with our finger movement, the child's affect brightened. The most minute movements combined with changes in sound engaged a multisensory experience.

The flute can also be a great cue for stretching and moving the body. In therapy sessions, as I play each long tone on the flute, I ask the group to breathe in and out with each change of note. As the participants exhale to one note, I ask them to drop one ear to the shoulder and to return their head to the center as they inhale, and as the pitch on the flute changes, I ask them to alternate sides. We tend to hold stress and tension in the trapezius muscles near the neck and shoulders. Especially for those of us living in a digital world and carrying out daily tasks by looking down at our digital devices, shoulder and neck pain is common. When we experience stress, there is a tightening of these muscles that can put them into spasms. Hunching forward brings strain and compression to the neck muscles, causing headaches, alignment issues, and muscle spasms. Stretching and relaxing with a musical cue can increase blood flow to the tense area. Ultimately, to gain better mobility in the neck and the body, it can be great to stretch slowly, using musical cues to change the movement or the side of the stretch. In addition to stretching the neck side to side, stretching the shoulders up and down and circling the wrists, hips, and ankles can bring great benefits to the central nervous system. Another helpful stretch is to stand tall in mountain pose, with feet and hips' distance apart. Clasping the hands low behind the back and taking a big stretch while raising the chest forward offers a wonderful stretch to the neck and trapezius muscles, all while opening the heart muscles and chest.

Breathing and listening to music while stretching offers soothing to the central nervous system. Inhaling deeply stimulates the sympathetic nervous system, and exhaling stimulates the parasympathetic nervous system. Exhaling into the flute, releasing long tones, engages the parasympathetic nervous system while creating beautiful music. Like the yin and yang in the heart, breath engages the same balanced interaction of systems. Breathing, singing, vocalizing, and playing wind instruments—these all give direction to the vibration of energy in our body and soothes the central nervous system.

Krystal L. Demaine

Companion Listening #5

"Lotus Flower" by Radiohead (2011)

Creative Exercise #5: Musical Pranayama

Sometimes the most important thing in a whole day is the rest we take between two deep breaths, or the turning inwards in prayer for five short minutes.
—Etty Hillesum, *An Interrupted* Life, *the Diaries, 1941–1943*

Musical pranayama, as I call it, integrates live musical sounds and music making with yogic breath work, prana (life energy) and yama (restraint). I always begin by teaching some different techniques that help engage the parasympathetic nervous system, bringing calm to the rapid heart, reducing anxiety, and, for some people, increasing breath support, which promotes greater fluency of speech. Practicing breathing with slow music (40–60 bpm), singing with music, playing flute, and engaging in yoga breathing techniques can all be beneficial.

What follows are some basic breathing exercises to practice. You may ask a partner to read these exercises out loud, or you may record yourself and practice while listening to the recording.

1. Four-Four Breathing: Breathe in for four counts, and breathe out for four counts. Repeat for 10 cycles.
2. Lion's Breath: Inhale through the nose for two counts, stick the tongue out, and exhale from the back of the throat like a lion yawning for four counts. Repeat for 10 cycles.
3. Alternate Nostril Breathing: In a seated position, bring the thumb and ring finger to the nose. Keeping your mouth closed, exhale completely and close the right nostril with the right thumb. Inhale through the left nostril, then close the left nostril with the ring finger. Remove the thumb and exhale through the right nostril. Inhale through the right nostril, and exhale through the left while alternating thumb and ring finger closing the respective nostril. Repeat for 10 cycles.

You may also practice gentle mindful breathing while listening to music with a slower tempo of 40–60 bpm. Instead of focusing on breathing, sit, listen, draw, daydream, and relax. Our bodies can entrain to slower

68

music, which relaxes our mind, breath, and body and induces calm. Here are some recommended music tracks below 60 bpm:

- "Something in the Way" by Nirvana (1991) 53 bpm
- "Say Something" by A Great Big World (2014) 48 bpm
- "Hallelujah" by Leonard Cohen (1984) 50 bpm
- *Moonlight* Sonata by Ludwig van Beethoven (1802) 60 bpm
- "Redemption Song" by Bob Marley and the Wailers (1980) 58 bpm
- "Lucy in the Sky with Diamonds" by the Beatles (1967) 47 bpm
- "Wish You Were Here" by Pink Floyd (1975) 59 bpm
- "Back to Bedlam" by James Blunt (2004) 47 bpm
- "Dazed and Confused" by Led Zeppelin (1969) 53 bpm

Breathing and Stretching with the Flute

If you have a Native American flute or a wooden flute that is easy to blow into, I suggest playing long tones. Inhale through your nose and then exhale through your mouth into the flute, blowing a single long tone with each exhale. As you play the flute, pair a neck stretch with each exhale. You can practice by gently dropping your ear to your shoulder with each exhale and then bringing the head to neutral with each inhale. You may also pair the stretches noted in chapter 5, such as circling the wrists, hips, and ankles and lifting and lowering the shoulders while inhaling and exhaling into the flute. With each exhale, play a long tone on the flute, stretching the neck and trapezius muscles, an area where we hold much tension and inflammation in the body. Play an ascending and then a descending five-note or eight-note scale.

References

Beitman, B. (2020, November 16). *The scarab: Jung created a coincidence with a coincidence.* Psychology Today. https://www.psychologytoday.com/us/blog/connecting-coincidence/202011/the-scarab-jung-created-coincidence-within-coincidence

Bolotnikov, K. (n.d.). *The many dialects of China.* Asia Society. https://asiasociety.org/china-learning-initiatives/many-dialects-china?page=1

Czycyk, A., Izak, M., & Paleczny, B. (2020). Characteristics of autonomic regulation of the heart function in musicians playing wind instruments. *Neurophysiology, 52*, 140–144. https://doi.org/10.1007/s11062-020-09863-4

Demaine, K. (2009). Melody versus rhythm: The relative roles of melody and rhythm in music therapy for two boys with autism. In S. L. Brooke (Ed.), *The use of creative therapies with autism spectrum disorders.* (pp. 200–223). Charles C. Thomas.

Demaine, K. (2015). Musical roots for healing: The five tone system in traditional Chinese medicine. In S. L. Brooke (Ed.), *Therapists Creating a Cultural Tapestry: Using the Creative Therapies Across Cultures* (pp. 154–169). Charles C. Thomas.

Harvard Health Publishing. (2020, July 6). *Relaxation techniques: Breath control helps quell errant stress response.* https://www.health.harvard.edu/mind-and-mood/relaxation-techniques-breath-control-helps-quell-errant-stress-response

Kogan, V., & Reiterer, S. (2021). Eros, beauty, and phon-aesthetic judgements of language sound. We like it flat and fast, but not melodious. Comparing phonetic and acoustic features of 16 European languages. *Frontiers in Human Neuroscience.* https://doi.org/10.3389/fnhum.2021.578594

Mathieu, W. A. (1991). *The listening book: Discovering your own music.* Shambhala Publications.

Turk, I. (1997). *Mousterian "bone flute" and other finds from Divje Babe I cave site in Slovenia.* Znanstvenoraziskovalni Center SAZU

Chapter 6

The Music Container

Music, uniquely among the arts, is both completely abstract and profoundly emotional. It has no power to represent anything particular or external, but it has a unique power to express inner states or feelings. Music can pierce the heart directly; it needs no mediation.
—Oliver Sacks, *Musicophilia: Tales of music and the brain*

The Human Need for Music

Music is a basic human need that offers salve and brings community in the most traumatic and horrific situations. On September 11, 2001, after extremist groups hijacked four US airplanes and killed thousands of innocent people, radio stations relied on music to provide calm and support. Talk radio stations switched their programming to classical music, and those that typically played intense musical genres opted for more soothing sounds. I was working in a nursing home for adults diagnosed with Alzheimer's disease on the morning of the attacks. The shock of what I was witnessing on the news, as nursing staff and therapists huddled with me around the TV in the solarium, made me want to drive home and be with my loved ones. Everyone was confused by the unbelievable sight, and it took time to sink in. Despite my strong pull to return home, I stayed at the nursing home and played music with the residents and their families.

During the COVID-19 pandemic, because of the high transmission risk of the virus, spread by water droplets just from talking within a six-foot radius, people around the world were restricted from playing musical instruments and singing in groups. Concerts and live performances came to a halt, and even school and college bands and ensemble groups were stopped. In March 2020, while the world was in quarantine, neighbors in Italy played instruments and sang songs from their apartment balconies and windows, together but separately (VanDerWerff, 2020). Psychologist Nisha Gupta (2020) deemed this creative union, or "musical solidarity," to have a "therapeutic ability to puncture the isolation of social distancing, to foster resiliency by lifting the collective spirit, and to move people's emotions toward spirited action—even if that action, in these circumstances, means staying home to save the lives of others" (pp. 595–596). The music making in Italy garnered worldwide attention and highlighted the natural urge for humans, as social creatures, to create and share.

Music informs our relationships and our connections to others as well as our physiological response to the rhythms of our environment. As music seeps into our crevices, it changes our frequency and vibration—allowing us to emote, transform, and engage in social awareness and connection. Music holds our thoughts, feelings, emotions, and our deepest secrets; it gives space to our pain. It is the container to explore our internal dialogue, the basin to embrace our celebrations, and the vessel to carry our grief. The music container allows us to feel pain and explore our fears, without judgment or even a reason why. Anthropologist Stephen Mithen (2006) has said that no society in the world exists without music. We can therefore see musical engagement as common to all human existence.

Music is good for the heart, the mind, and the soul. We have all felt how music can lift us. The use of music in healing is ancient and indigenous to many cultures across the globe and strikes a chord with patients, families, and scientists alike. Now, institutions across the world have begun to conduct scientific studies on the power of music. The National Institutes of Health have allocated millions of dollars in funding to research the benefits of music in treating neurologic conditions. Research labs across the world have investigated the use of music for children with autism and adults with neurologic conditions like stroke, Parkinson's disease, and Alzheimer's disease, in addition to studying how music evokes emotional responses.

Evidence-based, music-centered interventions have allowed music therapists to provide treatment in various settings, including hospitals, special education classrooms, mental health clinics, end-of-life care facilities, neonatal ICUs, and prisons. National and global organizations such as the Institute for Music and Neurologic Function, the Mariani Foundation, the American Music Therapy Association, as well as many, many others, hold annual symposia and conferences to disseminate the latest research on the power of music. At present, beyond the allied health profession of music therapy, sound healers, music thanatologists, and Kindermusik teachers all use music as a tool to help humans develop their desired potential.

With a lifelong music career, I write, say, think, sing, and read *music* more than anything else. To me, music is the tiny pulse that keeps us alive; its frequency courses through our bodies and aligns our atoms to solidify a home for the spirit where the soul resides. Music allows our human bodies to do necessary emotional work and intrinsic motor organization. Music is responsible for nearly every human developmental milestone, walking, balance, language development, and hand-eye coordination—none of which could occur without the pillars of rhythm and melody. Music invites a multisensory motor experience that provokes cognitive processes with the ability, even on the subconscious level, to engage the brain into the conscious world. Humans entrain to the pulse and tempo that surrounds us, linking breath and movement to a symphony of life.

Music in Utero

While I was pregnant with my son and working as a music therapist in 2012, I engaged with live music every day. I sang with groups of children and adults and played my guitar with it slung around my body. When I played the guitar and the sound resonated on my pregnant belly, I could feel my baby move and wiggle. I could also sense his stillness when the music stopped, almost as if he were patiently waiting for more. When I was near full term, I could feel my baby's body gravitating to a birth position, curled up and ready to move outside of the womb. His round, little bum, curled up just underneath my breasts at the top of my belly like a lump of dough waiting to rise, protruded from my body. With a little shift of the guitar to the side of my very full belly, I was able to accommodate this body growing inside of me. I was still able to play and sing in music therapy throughout the entire pregnancy. Music energized me and my son during our entire pregnancy together. While he was in utero, music became our secret language and playful interaction together—something I will always cherish.

Humans begin to learn about music in the womb. The gestating fetus can hear low-frequency sounds, such as the mother's heartbeat and voice, at around 18 weeks. After that time frame, auditory perception increases rapidly as the fetus begins to move and wiggle in response to the sounds it hears. According to Takayuki Nakata and Sandra Trehub (2004), the fetus is exposed to a myriad of musical stimuli, and the quality of emotive sounds, particularly singing, plays a role in the newborn's emotional development. By 26 weeks, the fetal heartbeat begins to respond to both musical and nonmusical sounds. According to Sangeeta Ullal-Gupta and colleagues (2013), the fetus by 33 weeks is able to breathe in tempo to music and by 38 weeks is able to respond to different genres and musical tempos through its movements and heart rate. Ullal-Gupta and colleagues suggest that fetal musical exposure plays an important role in the trajectory of the brain's wiring for music and of the musical mind.

Figure 5. *Interconnected*, 1992. Watercolor on etching, 6 x 9 in. Artist: Carol Pelletier. Reproduced by permission from Carol Pelletier.

Music also fosters relationship building in the womb. Sheila Woodward (2019) describes in the *Oxford Handbook of Singing* that an attachment connection is built between mother and fetus when a pregnant mother sings. Singing to a baby in the womb is a tradition that spans cultures and generations. According to Woodward, "Singing belongs to us all. It is not the exclusive privilege of highly educated musicians" (p. 536). When children are young, some parents and caregivers compose their own songs to aid in bath-time, feeding, and diaper-changing rituals. Music in this regard provides a sense of comfort and ritual as the child acclimates to their daily activities. Parents add a natural lilting melody to their phrases when performing these routines, and the natural singsong voice used to accompany them is termed "mother ease" or "parent ease."

Fetal heart rate and music were studied in 2018 by a group of researchers in Poland with 48 women in their third trimester of pregnancy (Gebuza et al., 2018). After the women listened to classical music, the researchers used the Sonicaid Team Standard Oxford Apparatus to record the fetuses' cardiographic activity. The researchers found that after the mother's music listening, there was a statistically significant increase in fetal heart rate and body movement and a decrease in uterine contractions, both integral markers of potential premature delivery. The research supports the use of recorded classical music in obstetrics and neonatal ICU settings to promote a calming space in an unnatural and potentially stressful environment.

Along similar lines, a 2016 study conducted in Taiwan researched the effects of music listening on sleep quality and anxiety among 121 pregnant women who reported sleep disturbances (Lui et al., 2016). Previous research had indicated that prenatal sleep disturbance is correlated to adverse pregnancy outcomes, such as preterm birth, delayed development, and obesity. In the study, half of the group (61 women) independently listened to lullabies, classical music, and crystal baby music (relaxation music designed for children) throughout the day. The other half, a control group of 60 expectant mothers, did not listen to music. All of the women maintained their prenatal exams and completed a pre-and post-test of the Pittsburg Sleep Quality Test and State-Trait Anxiety Inventory. A statistically significant difference was found among music-listening mothers, who experienced better-quality sleep and reduced stress and anxiety, factors that are generally linked to more comfortable and successful pregnancies.

Music and the Brain

Music and brain researcher Robert Zatorre describes the brain as hardwired for music. This means that, in essence, the brain is organized in a way that allows for pleasure through engaging in music, both listening and playing. Typically, the brain and body respond innately to music, inviting us to dance, move, sing, and emote (Zatorre, 2005). In the scholarly journal *Nature Neuroscience*, Salimpoor and colleagues (2011) write that music engages our reward pathways and that when we listen to music we like, music that creates the sensation of chills, our level of dopamine (a neurochemical responsible for movement regulation, mood, and attention) reaches its highest point. A vast number of research studies and books have described the neural processing of music and have highlighted the notion that music diffusely impacts the brain by tapping into numerous brain regions and cortices to promote physical, cognitive, and emotional functioning (Koelsch, 2012; Levitin, 2007; Sacks, 2007).

In 2008, I attended the Neurosciences and Music Conference III in Montreal, Canada. This was my first exposure to the big names in the field of music and neuroscience. I had recently completed a neurologic music therapy fellowship at Colorado State University and was invited to work as a clinical research assistant at the Music and Neuroimaging Laboratory with lab advisor, Gottfried Schlaug. It was Schlaug and colleagues who conducted one of the earliest studies on music and the brain in 2001. They researched musicians' brains to find out how they were structurally different from the brains of nonmusicians. The difference was identified especially in the corpus callosum, which is the band of ganglion fibers between the right and left hemispheres of the brain that allows these two regions to communicate. The researchers commented that music may enhance opportunities later in life for neuroplasticity, which had previously been thought possible only during early childhood when the brain is still developing. It is indeed possible to learn new skills at any point in our lives. Music learning is also beneficial for children's brains, and early music training promotes brain development and enhances language and mathematical abilities (Hyde et al., 2009).

While most people find music pleasing, some people find the music less than desirable. Neurologic differences such as synesthesia and amusia can completely change the aesthetic experience of music listening. Synesthesia, in which the stimulation of one sensory pathway stimulates another area, occurs in 2–4 percent of the human population. The word is derived from the Greek *synth* meaning "together" and *esthesia* meaning "perception." When a person with musical synesthesia hears a musical tone or sound, it can stimulate another sense, such as taste, sight, or texture. The most common form of musical synesthesia is chromosynesthesia, or sound-to-color synesthesia. In an article published in 2011 in *PLoS Biology*, David Brang and V. S. Ramachandran pointed to a genetic link for musical synesthesia. The majority of people who experience synesthesia acquire it after sensory or neurologic impairment or drug use; however, biological traits may explain this unique phenomenon. There is still more research to be done to explain why people have synesthesia and the benefits or implications of the condition.

Amusia is a form of tone deafness, either acquired or congenital, and it can make music listening almost unbearable. Researchers Krista Hyde and Isabella Peretz at the University of Montreal, Canada, pioneered the study of amusia beginning in the early 2000s. Amusia is an anomaly affecting about 4 percent of the US population and notably impacting music perception only when other intellectual abilities, including hearing and language understanding, are normal (Ayotte et al., 2002; Hyde & Peretz, 2004). What is unique about amusia is that perception of pitch can be intact while the perception of rhythm is missing. This fact indicates that there is a localized perceptional problem since rhythm and melody, as well as pitch discrimination, are located in different areas of the brain. A person with amusia may not be able to discern the difference between songs, and music may sound atrocious in its pitch or rhythm. In the book *Musicophilia*, Oliver Sacks (2007) describes a case of a person with amusia who perceived music as sounding like metal pots and pans crashing together. Now, that does not sound pleasing to the ear!

While not everyone may love music or perceive music in a pleasurable way, humans do experience an automatic response to music. For the neurologically impaired brain, music can serve as an alternative vehicle to promote speech and movement and to engage the memory system when these abilities have been lost. Through melody, pitch, rhythm, meter, and dynamics, music can stimulate humans in numerous ways; and I firmly believe that when it comes to treating a diversity of human needs, music offers the most comprehensive healing approach of any other rehabilitation therapy approach today.

Music and Emotion

The word *emotion*, which contains the word *motion*, indicates movement, flow, or vibration. There is movement in human emotions because of the variance and rapid fluctuation of emotional expression. It is rare for a person to maintain the same emotion throughout the day. Music can be a container that holds our fluctuating emotions without judgment, while at the same time inviting a deep expression of feelings. In addition, music can help convey emotions. The children's television personality Fred Rogers shared that when he was young, he was best able to convey his own emotions by playing the piano. Through the instrument, he could play happy, sad, or angry without having to use words to convey what he was feeling (Neville, 2018).

In the music therapy grief group that I lead for children, I ask each person, in turn, to choose a drum and play the true emotions that they feel inside. The person playing the drum can ask other group members to play along or just listen. The key to playing along is giving the children a chance to listen deeply, so they can meet (not imitate) the person in their sounds and feeling through musical dynamics and movement. Through their music playing, the children can guess the feelings and emotions the person is conveying. This nonverbal transfer of emotions through music offers a meaningful and noninvasive entry point into the person's emotional experience (Demaine, 2015). Children need a forum to express their emotions and a chance to share their stories and to be heard. One of the most valuable things we can do for one another is listening to our stories.

Music and neuroscience researcher Stefan Koelsch at the University of Bergen in Norway has conducted several studies on the neural implications of music and emotion. Working with functional magnetic resonance imaging, Koelsch (2014) was able to see when the emotional areas in the middle of the brain light up when exposed to certain kinds of music. These areas include the hippocampus, which is responsible for attachment-related emotions; the amygdala, which is responsible for our social-affective responses; the hypothalamus, which is responsible for body temperature, mood, and hunger; and the nucleus accumbens, also known as the reward center, which is responsible for the release of dopamine and serotonin.

Perhaps one of the most wonderful things about music is that it can evoke a myriad of emotions. Researchers at the University of California, Berkeley, surveyed emotional responses (28 categories) to music (40 samples) among 2,500 people across different cultures, including the United States and China, and mapped 13 emotional responses (Cowen et al., 2020). The responses included amusement, joy, eroticism, beauty, relaxation, sadness, dreaminess, triumph, anxiety, scariness, annoyance, defiance, and feeling pumped up. The map the researchers created is interactive and gives musical examples, the brain area activated by the music, and the emotion elicited. The *Emotions Evoked by Music* interactive map can be found at https://www.ocf.berkeley.edu/~acowen/music.html#modal.
Interestingly, the same emotional response to music was found across all the cultures that were assessed. The researchers thought that their findings might help those of us in medical treatment rooms to evoke positive moods as well as expand music-based search engines.

Sometimes when we hear songs from our past, it can conjure emotions and feelings, thoughts and memories, creating a thunderstorm of lights in the midbrain (the area that houses our emotional response), just as if we were at the place where we originally heard that song. From the ages of 8-13, I spent my summers amid the pine trees at Waukeela Camp for Girls in New Hampshire, where singing in groups was engrained in the camp culture. We sang in the dining hall during meals, in the showers, on hikes, at the campfire, and if our group took a day trip away from camp, we were asked to compose a song about our trip and to share it upon our return. Some of the songs at camp I had not heard anywhere else in my life. I later found out that many were composed at that camp and passed along over the years. The music that we are exposed to in our young lives can take on a very powerful role as we develop. Sometimes the music we find most comforting was sung to us or shared with our friends. Something I have found new comfort in is sacred chant and wordless melodies, for example, the niggun, wordless songs in the Jewish tradition, passed down for generations. While recordings of niggun likely exist, I have never heard original recordings; I have learned these melodies only from hearing my rabbi sing them. Whether familial, social, or spiritual, music can conjure memories and emotions that are held deep within in.

Music Soothes the Sympathetic

Music can be intrinsically meaningful for people with autism spectrum disorders (ASD). When I was working on my doctoral degree and even years earlier, I experienced a special connection with the children diagnosed with autism that I worked with. I felt a keen sensitivity and relatability to children with autism, and the way that I could connect to these children through music, art, and the senses was profound and meaningful to me. One of the diagnostic characteristics of ASD is the brain's challenge in processing sensory information, which results in the individual falling into a hypervigilant state. This state is an effect of the brain trying to process too much information; it results in a fight-or-flight response, where the person becomes stuck in the sympathetic. This stress response can happen to all people. We become stuck in this hypervigilant state, and we can miss social cues and the ability to make good decisions; self-regulation becomes a distant reach for our bodies and brains, and sometimes maladaptive behaviors result. With ASD in particular, this can mean difficulty regulating behavioral responses, leading to tantrums, aggression, panic, and sometimes psychosis. Being stuck in a sympathetic state for people with ASD shows similar features to anxiety and depression (Porges, 2011). Among the people who struggle with depression and anxiety that I have worked with in music therapy, some have said that when they had a psychotic experience, it caused them to black out. They did not remember what happened or it seemed like a blur, almost like a heavy night of drinking. When psychosis takes over the brain, the egregious acts that may occur may not even be recalled after the incident.

Neurochemicals exist in many bodily organs, not just the brain, because of the vagus nerve, which runs from the head to the gut. Therefore, it is important to consider how additional organs function in response to stress and sensory overload. Among people with ASD, gastrointestinal problems are prevalent, resulting in prescribed diets. Gluten-free and casein-free diets have been used to reduce inflammation and promote gut health. Since microbes in the gut are linked to neurologic function, researchers are eager to explore the relationship between gut and brain health (Griffiths & Mazmanian, 2018; Svoboda, 2020).

When a person becomes stuck in the sympathetic, there can be a sense of spiraling, like a computer that just will not load information. At that moment, the information that needs to be loaded is to cool down, or to tap into the rest and repair state of the parasympathetic. We can tell someone to stay calm, to breathe, to listen to their heart. But when this spiraling occurs, these verbal reminders may cause a person to become more hypervigilant. Music, as we know, has the power to cue the brain to tap into the parasympathetic, to remind us to listen, breathe into the heart, and to reach people when words cannot intervene.

Musical Entrainment and Attunement

The story of Huygens's pendulums gave us a sense that entrainment is grounded in rhythm and synchronicity. In music therapy, many neurologic-based treatment approaches rely specifically on musical rhythmic entrainment, or matching the movement to live or recorded rhythmic music with a steady tempo. This is also known as temporal synchronicity. "Temporal" has to do with timekeeping and the hearing region of the brain—the temporal lobe. When people engage in music-centered activities together, interpersonal musical entrainment occurs; we become coordinated with one another through temporal synchronicity (Clayton et al., 2020). Because music is virtually everywhere in our modern-day civilization, musical entrainment is something that our bodies are familiar with. When we hear music, we tend to swing our arms and walk to its beat. We may find ourselves in the grocery store moving to the tempo of the music coming in through the speakers. According to early research conducted by Philip Kotler in the 1970s, music may provoke people in grocery stores to buy more by creating a stimulating and enjoyable atmosphere in which people want to spend time (Kotler, 1973). Many commercial spaces play music to induce calm or focus by entraining body movements. We find that places like yoga studios play more calming music, 50 bpm or less, while a gym might play more vigorous up-tempo music. Faster-tempo music has been found to increase endurance and encourage high-intensity workouts, such as running or other cardio activities (Patania et al., 2020).

Runners have told me that they rely on music to keep them engaged in the activity. The connection between the rhythm of music, the heartbeat, and the pacing when running can feel magical for runners. My runner friends have reported that the music motivates them, that moving to the beat helps them to reach a state of flow, the ingredient for the ultimate runner's high—a state of euphoria. Similarly, in the military, singing helps keep the pace when marching, unifying the group in synchronicity.

When we play music with other people, interpersonal musical entrainment takes over us; there begins to be a flow like in the runner's high. When we first start to learn how to play a musical instrument, we focus on how we sound and if we are playing the correct notes. At some point, we let go of our self-critique and become aware of how the group sounds together and its musical cohesion. The more we play music with that group, the more we become in synchrony with one another. Music making invites a nonverbal dialogue in which we yield to the flow of the group, especially when the music is improvised.

In 2017 I gave a couple of workshops at the Latin American Music Therapy Symposium in Panama. My former Berklee College of Music professor, Colin Lee was also presenting, and on the topics of aesthetic music therapy and improvisation. I hadn't seen Colin since he left his teaching position at Berklee in 1999 and our reunion felt welcome and tender. During his workshop, he invited me to the floor to participate in a 1:1 music demonstration. Colin asked me to choose an instrument to play along with him while he played the piano. I chose a djembe drum. My son, three years old at the time, sat in the front row of the audience with his eyes laser-focused on the scene. I sat in a chair with the drum in front of me. Colin signaled me to start playing play the drum. I began to tap on the head of the drum slowly and cautiously while Colin matched my dynamics with the piano (a great example of the music therapy iso principle as discussed earlier). As the sound progressed, I played louder and then faster. Colin's piano playing met me in every change with sound, shape, and emotion in a way that felt like I was being heard and understood more than I have ever felt in my life. We played together for about five minutes and when the music finally came to a pause, we stood up next to each other to share the experience and translate it into words for the audience. But when Colin asked how I was feeling I started to cry. Tears automatically streamed down my face, and I said, "I haven't been heard like that in a long time —maybe never." I wasn't sure if it was the fact that I hadn't seen Colin in so many years or that the music stimulated some emotions in me, but that musical attunement experience is one that will carry with me for the rest of my life.

Whether we are listening to the lilting 60 bpm of Beethoven's *Moonlight* Sonata or the 139 bpm of Gorillaz's "Feel Good Inc.," our body, heart, and emotion wants to move and entrain to the tempo. Some music changes tempo in the middle of the song, as does "Bubble House" by Medeski Martin and Wood, which is a great example of ascending and descending tempos to move and dance to. Whatever the music's tempo, our body knows how to acclimate, how to tune in, and how to follow. It is our capacity for musical entrainment and the vibrations that we share as humans that allow us to connect more deeply to one another and the frequencies of the universe. Being held in music can allow for a sense of belongingness, connection, and relational understanding that goes beyond words. It is our sensing of the music within —the pulse, that allows us to learn how to walk, to talk, and to relate others. Tuning into the pulse of the heart, finding the music of our life, and curating our musical soundtrack will allow a deep attunement to the self and offer a doorway to musical entrainment.

Companion Listening #6

"Fix You" by Coldplay (2005)

Creative Exercise #6: Musical Life Review

This creative exercise asks you to catalog the music that has played a role in your life. We hear music throughout our daily lives in various locations, places, and moments. Music can carry us from the most joyful experiences to the most challenging ones. Each song we hear can conjure an image, a memory, or a sensation embedded in our bodies. Creating a musical life review will allow you to revisit the stories of your life using music as a connective thread. Think of this as creating a soundtrack to tell the story of your life from your earliest musical memory to the present. Begin with your childhood and progress onward from there. If you cannot think of the songs on your own, you may choose to ask your friends, family members, or people who know you to perhaps rekindle the music that you listened to together. With every song you choose, include a brief note about the memory, image, or story that relates to the song. Over the years you may continue to add to your soundtrack. Keep it in a safe place so that you may share it with those who are important to you.

My musical life review (selection):
- *Going Quackers* by Donald Duck, Willio, and Phillio (1980). This is the first record album I remember owning and loving.
- "Little Wing" by Jimi Hendrix (1967). This was my favorite song from Dad's record collection.
- Flute Concerto in D Minor (*La Notte*) by Antonio Vivaldi (1719). This composition reminds me of my first flute, which my parents bought for me through a newspaper advertisement for $100 in 1987.
- "Mrs. Robinson" by Simon and Garfunkel (1968). This song reminds me of car rides to camp in New Hampshire during my youth (1987–1992).
- "Even Flow" by Pearl Jam (1992). This song was the epitome of alternative rock and was a major part of my identity development during adolescence. It informed my

hairstyle and dress and reminds me of my attire at the time, flannel shirts and jeans ripped jeans at the knees.

- "Tax Man" by the Beatles (1966). This was the first song that my dad taught me to play on the bass guitar when I was 15 years old. He taught it to me on a blond Hofner bass guitar, the same make of guitar that Paul McCartney plays.
- "Waste" by Phish (1966). This song reminds me of the many, many Phish concerts I attended in the 1990s with my best friend, Maggie, and my sisters.
- "Blue in Green" by Miles Davis (1959). This song reminds me of relaxing with my friends at Berklee College of Music and the time that I transcribed all of Miles Davis's solos from the entire *Kind of Blue* album.
- "Forever" by Ben Harper (1994). This song inspired me to write my own songs and perform them on acoustic guitar at open mic nights and in coffee shops, pubs, and restaurants.
- "Fake Plastic Trees" by Radiohead (1995). This song became the anthem of my 20s and 30s and evokes relationships, love, heartache, and heartbreak.
- "Clandestino" by Manu Chao (2000). This song reminds me of trips to Mexico, love, loss, and growth.
- "Ong Namo" performed by Snatam Kaur (2004). I listened to this traditional chant while birthing my son. It has also been the most healing music since the loss of my father, and it was Snatam Kaur's opening song when I saw her perform after my father died. This song connects me to new life, life transition, life loss, and rebirth.
- "Rainbow Connection" by Kermit the Frog (1979). This song, from *The Muppet Movie*, reminds me of my son, and we like to sing it together.

References

Ayotte, J., Peretz, I., & Hyde, K. (2002). Congenital amusia: A group study of adults afflicted with a music-specific disorder. *Brain*, *125*, 238–251.

Brang, D., & Ramachandran, V. S. (2011). Survival of the synesthesia gene: Why do people hear colors and taste words? *PLoS Biology*, *9*(11). https://doi.org//10.1371/journal.pbio.1001205

Clayton, M., Jakubowski, K., Eerola, T., Keller, P., Camurri, A., Volpe, G., & Alborno, P. (2020). Interpersonal entrainment in music performance: Theory, method, and model. *Music Perception*, 38(2), 136–194. https://doi.org/10.1525/mp.2020.38.2.136

Cowen, A. S., Fang, X., Suter, D., & Keltner, D. (2020). What music makes us feel: At least 13 dimensions organize subjective experiences associated with music across different cultures. *Proceedings of the National Academy of Sciences*, *117*(4), 1924–1934. https://doi.org/10.1073/pnas.1910704117

Demaine, K. (2015). These are my memories of you: The use of music therapy with children's grief support groups. In S. L. Brooke & D. Miraglia (Eds.), *Using the creative therapies to cope with grief and loss* (pp. 180–196). Charles C. Thomas.

Gebuza, G., Saleska, M., Kazmierczak, M., Mieczkowska, E., & Gierszewska, M. (2018). The effect of music on cardiac activity of a fetus in a cardiotocoghraphic examination. *Advances in Clinical Experimental Medicine*, *27*(5), 615–621.

Griffiths, J. A., & Mazmanian, S. K. (2018). Emerging evidence linking the gut microbiome to neurologic disorders. *Genome Medicine*, *10*(98). https://doi.org/10.1186/s13073-018-0609-3

Gupta, N. (2020). Singing away the social distancing blues: Art therapy in a time of Coronavirus. *Journal of Humanistic Psychology*, *60*(5), 593–603.

Hyde K. L., & Peretz, I. (2004). Brains that are out of tune but in time. *Psychological Science*, *15*(5), 356–360. https://doi.org//10.1111/j.0956-7976.2004.00683.x

Hyde, K. L., Lerch, J., Norton, A., Forgeard, M., Winner, E., Evans, C. A., & Schlaug, G. (2009). Musical training shapes structural development. *Journal of Neurosciences: The Official Journal of the Society for Neuroscience*, *29*(10), 3019-3025.

Koelsch, S. (2012) *Brain and music*. Wiley-Blackwell.

Koelsch, S. (2014). Brain correlates of music-evoked emotions. *Nature Reviews Neuroscience*, *15*, 170–180.

Kotler, P. (1973). Atmospherics as a marketing tool. *Journal of Retailing*, *49*(4), 48–64.

Levitin, D. J. (2007). *This is your brain on music: The science of the human obsession.* Penguin Random House.

Lui, Y., Lee, C. S., Yu, C., & Chen, C. (2016). Effects of music listening on stress, anxiety, and sleep quality for sleep-disturbed pregnant women. *Women and Health, 56*(3), 296–311.

Mithen, S. (2006). *The singing Neanderthals.* Harvard University Press.

Nakata, T., & Trehub, S. E. (2004). Infants' responsiveness to maternal speech and singing. *Infant Behavior and Development, 27,* 455–464. https://doi.org/10.1016/j.infbeh.2004.03.002

Neville, M. (Director). (2018). *Won't you be my neighbor* [Film]. Tremolo Productions.

Patania, V. P., Padulo, J., Iuliano, E., Ardigò, L. P., Čular, D., Miletić, A., & De Giorgio, A. (2020). The psychophysiological effects of different tempo music on endurance versus high-intensity performances. *Frontiers in Psychology,* 11. https://doi.org//10.3389/fpsyg.2020.00074

Porges, S. W. (2011). *The polyvagal theory: Neurophysiological foundations of emotions, attachment, communication, and self-regulation.* W. W. Norton.

Sacks, O. (2007). *Musicophilia: Tales of music and the brain.* Knopf.

Salimpoor, V. N., Benovoy, M., Larcher, K., Dagher, A., & Zatorre, R. (2011). Anatomically distinct dopamine release during anticipation and experience of peak emotion to music. *Nature Neuroscience, 14*(2), 257-262.

Schlaug, G. (2001). The brain of musicians. A model for functional and structural adaptation. *Annals of the New York Academy of Sciences, 6*(930), 281–299.

Svoboda, E. (2020, January). Could the gut microbe be linked to autism? *Nature Outlook: The Gut Microbe, 577,* S14–S15. https://doi.org/10.1038/d41586-020-00198-y

Ullal-Gupta, S., Vanden Bosch der Nederlanden, V., Tichko, P., Lahav, A., & Hannon, E. (2013). Linking prenatal experience to the emerging musical mind. *Frontiers in Systems Neuroscience, 7*(48). https://doi.org//10.3389/fnsys.2013.00048

VanDerWerff, E. (2020, March 13). *Quarantined Italians are singing their hearts out. It's beautiful.* Vox. https://www.vox.com/culture/2020/3/13/21179293/coronavirus-italy-covid19-music-balconies-sing

Woodward, S. (2019). Fetal, neonatal, and early infant experiences of maternal singing. In D. Howard, J. Nix, & G. Welch (Eds.),

The Oxford handbook of singing (pp. 431–453). Oxford University Press.

Zatorre, R. (2005) Music, the food of neuroscience? *Nature, 434,* 312–315.

Chapter 7

The Roots to Our Rhythm

The holiest of all holidays are those
Kept by ourselves in silence and apart;
The secret anniversaries of the heart.
—Henry Wadsworth Longfellow, *Secret Anniversaries of the Heart*

Musical Identity

Music lies within the very essence of an individual's identity, from the rhythmic beat of the heart to music embedded by ancestors, as well as the rhythms and sounds we are exposed to in our development. Adolescence, in particular, is a time of forging the critical part of the identity that shapes how we relate to others as adults. Around 2003, I was working with adolescents at a residential high school. Many of the students were dealing with extreme anxiety or depression, and music was the best way for them to find a space of calm and to connect with others. Many teens in the group had criminal records, trauma, and lifelong mental health challenges. Nearly all had no relationship with their family of origin.

These music therapy groups involved songwriting and poem writing, instrument playing, audio recording, lyric analysis, music relaxation, art making, and some yoga. At the beginning of each session, one of the teens shared a song with everyone. The students brought different genres of music. Though the majority of the music was aggressive in nature, such as heavy metal and death metal, some students brought lighter pop music. In addition to making music, the students created drawings, collages, or mandalas. Art offered another language for the students to share the voice of their music and how they related to it. One student who loved heavy metal and melancholy music explained that this type of music helped him when he was feeling depressed, yet he also said that the music sometimes made him more depressed and made him feel stuck. Music can be a place to hold our emotions, but sometimes if we linger in a single emotional place for a little too long, the emotions deepen and the neurochemical balance can become difficult to manage resulting in a rut and maybe resulting in prolonged anxiety or even depression. It is natural and important for human emotions to fluctuate a little throughout the day; sometimes we feel sad and other times, happy or lonely and then totally content. Groupwork and the sharing of emotions through creative expression can offer a sense of belongingness, and that sense of belongingness can promote resiliency. We need to build tools for resilience, to know how to move from feeling frustrated to calm. Music was a big part of these teens' identity and offered a salve when they were struggling; one said that music was something they could not live without. This group helped the students to find connection and group cohesion, explore expressive identity, and find a sense of self that could help them cultivate the roots of their own lives simply by exploring words, rhythms, and sounds. Group members found compassion, inner coherence, and common ground; and their mental health concerns seemed to disappear.

Douglas Lonie (2009), a graduate student at the University of Glasgow, was curious to know how musical identity played a role in emotional well-being during the transition from adolescence to adulthood. Lonie analyzed a data set from an earlier longitudinal study about adolescent music identity and its implications on adult behavior; he then synthesized that study with a new group of 18 participants. Both sets of research yielded the same finding—that musical preference changes during the transition from adolescence into adulthood. In addition, Lonie found that participants who identified or related more with music during their youth also had riskier health behaviors during that period. However, in adulthood, those same people were more likely to use music for personal health and wellness reasons. On the other side of the coin, those who did not consider music significant earlier in life were less likely to engage in risky health behaviors; and they also did not use music as a source of health and well-being later in life. Lonie concluded that music does play a role in health and behavioral outcomes in youth but also that musical preferences, along with the health-related impacts of music use, may change during adulthood.

Quite often, we think of the music we listen to as an expression of our personality or identity. In 2003, Peter Rentfrow and Samuel Gosling at the University of Texas at Austin identified five musical personality types. They collected data from several thousand undergraduate students using the Short Test of Music Preferences, which assesses preferences in music genres. They also analyzed the music collected by students who used Internet file-sharing services. They found that the participants who liked "upbeat and conventional" music scored high in extraversion and political conservatism. Those who preferred "reflective and complex" music were more open and politically liberal and had higher verbal abilities. How we relate to music can inform our personality, the way we live our lives, and how we connect and relate to others.

Musical Tendrils

Climbing plants grow tendrils, tiny appendages that stretch outward, seeking support from objects nearby. These tendrils are what give the plant its connections to others. Once I started to play music, my metaphorical tendrils began to grow and I became connected to the world. Music allowed me to find my place and identity, bond with others, and communicate my voice. I was often described as a shy child, which was likely inherited. I spent the majority of my time alone in my bedroom, where posters of fractals and the California Raisins were pinned on the walls, cassette tapes mounded in random piles on the floor. I was more inclined to stay in the safe, cozy sphere of solitude within my childhood home than to be out looking for friends. I spent hours drawing pictures, listening to music, and building Lego lands with my sisters in our basement. I sustained a creative drawing habit, producing stacks of sketchbooks with drawings and designs of comic book characters, cities, and maps. I also had a proclivity for magic and healing. I kept my perpetually growing magic crystal kit under my desk, which was covered with books on auras, palmistry, crystals, the healing power of music, and tarot cards. I was especially inclined to collect things, in part because of my father and grandfather, who were collectors of coins, baseball cards, and musical instruments. I was perfectly happy in the space of my home, relying on my parents and sisters for the majority of my socialization.

Since before I can recall, my parents owned a small business: a giftshop in Rockport, Massachusetts, the Bearskin Neck Country Store, which they operated on a seasonal calendar. Throughout my youth, I hung out on Bearskin Neck, the main drag in Rockport. During the busy summer season, Mom and Dad worked in their shop for more than 15 hours a day, while my sisters and I stayed with a sitter. One of my most vivid memories of those summers was when I asked my dad why he thought I was so shy, and reclusive really. Dad said it was because he and Mom were not able to socialize me very well. My father's rationale for my timid nature has always conjured for me an image of a poorly socialized dog with a great deal of anxiety, back hunched over, head turned back, and struggling to pull from anyone who came near. In fact, at age three, I recall sitting in my stroller, shying away from social interactions, covering my face, and crying when anyone other than my parents attempted to approach me. I also remember running away, when new adults sang "Happy Birthday" to me at the age of five (just as my son did when the chorus of the same song rang out at his fifth-year party).

As the oldest daughter of three girls, I was relatively unique among my siblings with my reserved nature. Later, I came to find out that being around people charges my heart, my emotions, and my capacity to love. At heart, I am an extrovert, recharged by teaching in the classroom and playing music with people. Music played a role in developing my identity, coming out of my shyness, healing my heart, and connecting with others. It was music that allowed me to blossom.

Around the age of four, I received my first record player. It was enclosed in a tan hard plastic case with a handle, and I carried it up and down Bearskin Neck like it was my gig bag. My favorite record was *Going Quackers* by Donald Duck, though my dad also let me play and listen to his record collection, which he kept organized in two old and sturdy wooden wine boxes. My father, a musician by training and by heart, introduced me to listening to and playing music. Though I was quiet and reserved in the early days, playing music was what got me on the stage and allowed me to share with others and engage socially.

Stephen Shore, an adult person with autism, was considered as a child to be nonverbal and to have fixed preoccupied interests, with difficulty associating with others. He developed a passion for music and ultimately earned bachelor's and master's degrees in music education and a doctoral degree in special education, and he is now a professor of special education at Adelphi University (Shore, 2020). At the Autism Forum in April 2012, Shore explained, "Some of the key aspects to my development were that my parents emphasized music, movement, sensory integration, narration, and imitation; they started to imitate me, and once they did that, I became aware in my environment!"

While there is a commonality in how music makes us feel, musical abilities are cultivated through study, inherited through our genes, or absorbed from our environment. Research has shown that both genetics and environment play a role in musical abilities (Tan et al., 2014). Our sense of rhythm and melody may be pumped into our bloodlines, but like all heritable behaviors, they may not always exist without the culture and environment that we live in. The heritable bond that my father and I shared was through music. There is nothing that makes me more satisfied and fulfilled than playing music with other people. Not every family is as musical as the Jackson 5, Hanson, or the Jonas brothers—my family certainly was not. What is important, though, is to carry that music with you and to share it with future generations.

Some studies have pointed to certain cultures having higher musical abilities, specifically having an absolute or perfect pitch, Most research studies that have to do with musical skills are based on absolute pitch, which is determined by the ability to identify and replicate music notes and pitches. Ashkenazi Jews are among those with a high prevalence of absolute pitch, which some have suggested is due to a strong tradition of early musical liturgical training—reading the Torah in Hebrew. However, it has also been noted that people of this descent, even outside of the liturgical environment, often begin musical training early, from around the age of three or four, and continue that musical study (Baharloo et al., 1998).

As my musical interests developed and I started to play music with other people, I gained a broader perspective on the world. It was music that opened my heart to invite others into my life and afforded me a career. Music can offer the tendrils to grow and the space to make new connections, allowing us to unfold and expand our world and deepen our identity. And sometimes it can give us a place to grow new roots, find grounding, and begin to explore the rhythm of our heart.

The Tree

Trees offer a wonderful metaphor for exploring the inner and outer worlds of the human body's relationships with ancestors. It can afford us a chance to explore what can be seen and unseen from a new perspective. The care for our bodies and the care of forests and trees go hand in hand. Trees absorb carbon dioxide from the environment, allowing for fresher and cleaner air. But because of human activity and deforestation, carbon dioxide levels are on the rise. According to NASA (2021), carbon dioxide levels have risen 48 percent since 1850 mainly due to the industrial revolution. This is more than what was produced in the 20,000 years prior.

In Jewish culture, there is an annual celebration of the trees, Tu b' Shvat, which is translated as "New Year of the Trees." This day celebrates ecological awareness, and typically, people plant new trees and show care for all things tree related, enjoying the fruits of In the book *The Hidden Life of Trees*, German forestry researcher Peter Wohlleben (2017) describes the forest as a social network—with trees silently communicating, arguing, nourishing, sharing, and disseminating information to each other. The principal part of a tree's life takes place underground in its roots through a network of fungi that links every tree in a forest. The roots of trees extend out as far as four times further than their height, and usually, the tallest trees have the shallowest root system. Imagine your network of relationships in life as the roots of a tree, connecting you with work colleagues, family, friends, and others. Sometimes these roots can pop through the earth like bulgy veins, or they can be hidden deep in the earth, way out of view.

Figure 6. *Tree #355*, 2020. Watercolor on paper, 5.8 x 8.3 in. Artist: Tamar Reva Einstein. Reproduced by permission from Tamar Reva Einstein.

Putting Down Roots

The roots of a family are often unknown or misunderstood. Sometimes roots can be hidden and never discussed—sometimes roots are bulging or wounded. In my family, there has been some uncertainty about the roots of my last name, Demaine. I am clear in knowing that the name is derived from the French word *demain*, which means tomorrow, but as far as my family knows, no one in our lineage was of French origin. When I was growing up, I heard that my last name was a given name, by a person who protected my family from Jewish persecution in eastern Europe during the early 1900s. Another thing I heard was that when my ancestors immigrated to the United States, they, of their own accord, changed their last name to avoid being recognized as Jewish and being maltreated. I also heard rumors that my paternal grandmother Esther changed the name simply because she adored the French language.

Shortly after my paternal grandfather died in February 2004, my father found Grandpa's birth certificate and sought out the truth behind our last name. My grandfather's birth certificate read Robert Samuel Bloom (not Demaine). He was a violinist and salesman, born in Boston, Massachusetts, on August 2, 1916, to Harry Bloom and Lena Snyder of Courland, Russia (now in Latvia). My grandfather had only an eighth-grade education, yet he wrote and told stories with eloquence; he was as smart as he was witty. My father was able to locate documents and letters, death certificates, titles, and newspaper articles about our family. By combing through documents, he found out that, according to the 1910 US census, my great-great-grandparents Joseph and Minnie Bloom immigrated with their family to America in 1887. The family members who came with them were my great-grandfather Harry Bloom (aged 17), his brother Simon (aged 14), his older sister Annie (aged 22), and her husband Harry Shanbar (aged 23). My great-grandfather became a US citizen in 1935, followed by my great-grandmother, Lena, in 1939, both under the surname Bloom. Just one year later, on July 13, 1940, their son and my grandfather Robert S. Demaine (not Bloom) married my grandmother Esther Freedman.

Robert was the one responsible for changing the family name from Bloom to Demaine in 1940, just after his parents became US citizens. When my grandparents married in 1940, my grandmother, a poet and oil painter, had already received a bachelor's degree in literature from Boston College; my grandfather was a salesman and violinist who had already done a stint in the Coast Guard. We do not truly know why my paternal grandfather changed the family name, but the decision was likely due to anti-Semitism, especially related to Grandpa's being a salesman and wanting to somewhat conceal his

Jewish identity. Or perhaps, along similar lines, as the family was putting down roots in Boston, they wanted the newly American Harry and Lena (my great-grandparents) and the generations of family to come to have a fully fresh start.

When it comes to building the roots of our musical lives, the source that nourishes our growth does not have to come from our biological family, our blood relatives, or our bloodlines. Our musical roots may come from nonfamilial surroundings or discoveries within our soul. Just one year before my favorite jazz musician Miles Davis died, he published a wonderful autobiography. Aside from my father, Davis has been one of my greatest musical influences, and to this day, I consider Miles Davis my first jazz teacher. In the book *Miles: The Autobiography*, Davis says, "For me, music has been my life, and musicians I have known and loved and grown from have become my family. My blood family is my family because of my parents, relatives, and blood. But for me, my family are the people I associate with in my profession—other artists, musicians, poets, painters, dancers, and writers—but not critics" (Davis & Troupe, 1990, p. 410).

The musician and Sufi practitioner Fred Johnson began developing his musical roots through his journey into Sufi mysticism. In November 2019, when Fred visited my classroom to speak to the students about music and dance, he recounted his life before the age of five, a chaotic time when he was swiftly moved between various foster homes. He noticed that at that crucial time of development as a child, sound was what grounded his emotions—and his body. Sound guided and nurtured him and was an ever-present companion. As he grew older and began to talk and discover language, he began to express himself through singing. The ability to sing, dance, and communicate through sound and movement, Fred said, allowed him to find calm in his tumultuous young world. At 67 years old, Fred came to discover that his life's journey has been one of finding inner wholeness through the frequency of sounds and understanding the mystery of life about where he came from.

> *The place for which you have been searching is always the place in which we have secretly been standing.*
> —Devon Spier, *Heart Map and the Song of Our Ancestors*

Companion Listening #7

"The Song of Your Heart" by Peter Kater and Snatam Kaur (2012)

Creative Exercise #7: Roots and Trees

It is time to channel your inner tree. Find a journal to write in and art materials of your choosing—clay, ink, paint, beads, wire, blocks. You could instead use objects for assemblage or draw in the sand.

To bring the tree to the mind's eye, you can begin by looking at trees. Perhaps take a walk in the forest or look at photographs or artwork of trees. Consider the give-and-take with trees: trees take nutrients from the soil and in turn provide fresh air for humans to breathe; wood for fuel, paper, and building; fruit to eat; and a soothing sound as leaves rustle in a soft breeze.

Begin to visualize yourself as a tree. Become grounded into the floor, feet rooted like the roots of a tree in the soil. Feel your toes move, wiggle, or grip the soil. The soil is the common ground for all life. Visualize the roots of the tree: determine their shape, their thickness, their depth beyond the Earth's crust, and their interconnectedness to one another, in ways both visible and invisible. Notice how you begin to move or sway in the breeze, how the air, the sun, and the mist feel.

Continue with the visualization, starting from the roots (feet) up to the top of your tree (head). You may consider recording yourself slowly reading the prompts and using the recording to perform the visualization, or you might ask someone to read it aloud for you.

- Roots (feet): Notice how deep or wide your roots travel, what those roots reach toward, and if they connect with any others.
- Trunk and bark (legs, torso, and skin): Notice how wide the trunk is, how hollow or thick, the feel of the bark, and how rough, smooth, or flaky. Notice the visitors on the tree bark—critters, carvings, bugs, or worms. Notice the rings tightly woven together inside, wide, smooth, or contoured. Perhaps your trunk is two trees grafted together; perhaps one is more robust.
- Branches (arms): Notice the thickness of your branches, their length, where they have been cut and where they grow wild, and where the branch breaks and starts a new branch.

- Twigs and tendrils (fingers): Notice the length and movement of the twigs and tendrils, the curves, the angles, and how they move toward the sun or curl in at night.
- Fruit (head): Notice the buds, blossoms, and fruit that the tree bears. Notice if the fruit is edible, its color, its shape and if it reproduces each year.
- Leaves (hair): Notice the shape and form of the leaves—smooth, jagged, small, large, veiny, opaque, red, green, orange, plasticky, frail.

After your visualization, begin to create a representation of your tree using your art materials. Perhaps sculpt an abstract tree out of clay or inscribe it in the sand. Make a tree out of wire and beads, or create a drawing with oil pastels. Creating art is a way of making the mentally visualized experience more tangible.

After you create your art, begin to translate the tree into written language. Write in your journal a description of your tree and what the tree looks like or feels like. Describe the elements of the tree—the roots, the bark, what is on the inside, and the fruits the tree bears. Now consider where the tree is located in the world and if are there trees around to communicate with. Consider what your tree takes and gives from the community and environment where it is rooted. Consider how the tree reacts in particular situations, in a rainstorm, extreme winds, or the heat of the blazing sun.

Now as you write in your journal, consider how your own life is represented by this tree. Like the tree, there is often no choice as to where your roots will grow. Consider how your life would be if you could choose your roots, whom you would choose to connect with, and the depth of communication with those contacts. Consider if your roots are peering out of the soil or are staying hidden. Also, consider how the bark protects the tree from harm and what you do with your own body to make it less permeable to harmful influences. Consider what the bearing of fruit means to you, how far your branches reach, and what you are reaching for. Finally, if you have leaves, consider their significance, how you would let your leaves fall, and how this informs your transitions with the seasons of life.

References

Baharloo, S., Johnston, P. A., Service, S. K., Gitschier, J., & Freimer, N. B. (1998). Absolute pitch: An approach for identification of genetic and nongenetic components. *American Journal of Human Genetics, 62*(2), 224–231.

Davis, M., & Troupe, Q. (1990). *Miles: The autobiography.* Simon and Schuster.

Lonie, D. (2009). Musical identities and health over the youth–adult transition [Unpublished doctoral dissertation]. University of Glasgow.

NASA (National Aeronautics and Space Administration). (April, 2021). *Carbon dioxide.* https://climate.nasa.gov/vital-signs/carbon-dioxide/

Rentfrow, P. J., & Gosling S. D. (2003). The do re mi's of everyday life: The structure of personality correlates of music preferences. *Journal of Personality and Social Psychology, 84*(6), 1236-1256.

Shore, S. (2020). *About Dr. Stephen Shore.* https://drstephenshore.com/about-stephen

Tan, Y. T., McPherson, G. E., Peretz, I., Berkovic, S., & Wilson, S. (2014). The genetic basis of music ability. *Frontiers in Psychology, 5*, 658. https://doi.org//10.3389/fpsyg.2014.00658

Wohlleben, P. (2017). *The hidden life of trees.* William Collins.

Chapter 8

The Heart of Our Ancestors

To see a World in a Grain of Sand and a Heaven in a Wild Flower
Hold Infinity in the palm of your hand and Eternity in an hour
—William Blake, *Auguries of Innocence*

Lines in the Hand

Our ancestors are always with us. Buddhist monk Thich Nhat Hanh said, "If you look deeply into the palm of your hand, you will see your parents and all generations of your ancestors. All of them are alive in this moment. Each is present in your body. You are the continuation of each of these people" (2006, p. 74). In some cultures, ancestors can come from the spiritual realm and may not be human; they can exist in nature, embodied in a tree or a plant. When I began writing this book, I wanted to include a photograph of the hands of the living members of my family, specifically my son, me, and my parents. I wanted to capture the lines in the palms of our hands. Every time I visited my parents' apartment, I planned to take a picture, and each time when I returned home, I realized that I had forgotten. It was important for me to see the lines in our hands together, to compare and study them. Ultimately, on the day that my father was dying in the hospital, I was able to capture a photograph of my mother, my son, and me holding Dad's hand (shown below).

Fingers and hands are uniquely identifiable, and hand identification has helped locate missing people and track criminals. We use fingerprint and hand geometry identification to access bank accounts, locked doors, and cell phones. Palm readers study the entire hand, including the palm, nails, fingers, length, depth of lines, and markings, and they use these features to foretell a person's future.

My father and I had similar hands. He described our hands as vascular; our veins protruded in a way that seemed unique and bonding to me. The palms of our hands showed deep, worn lines—crevices that seemed to tell stories and unwritten experiences. I remember my dad holding his hand up to mine, palm to palm, measuring the size of our hands together. He said that my hands were small, and he helped me buy smaller guitars for music therapy, so my little hands were able to

99

wrap around the neck. The three-quarter-size Larrivée guitar and the Little Martin guitar made music therapy sessions less cumbersome. As a young girl, I imagined the blood pumping through the veins in my hand as the same blood that pumped through our ancestors—multiple generations joining together like rivers, streams, and tributaries, intersecting and taking what we need, leaving behind what we do not need as we use our hands to work and make music. I often watched my father play his upright bass guitar, with his hand moving on the thick acoustic strings. I wondered how my grandfather's hands looked playing the violin and how my great-grandparents and my great-great-parents looked as they created their music.

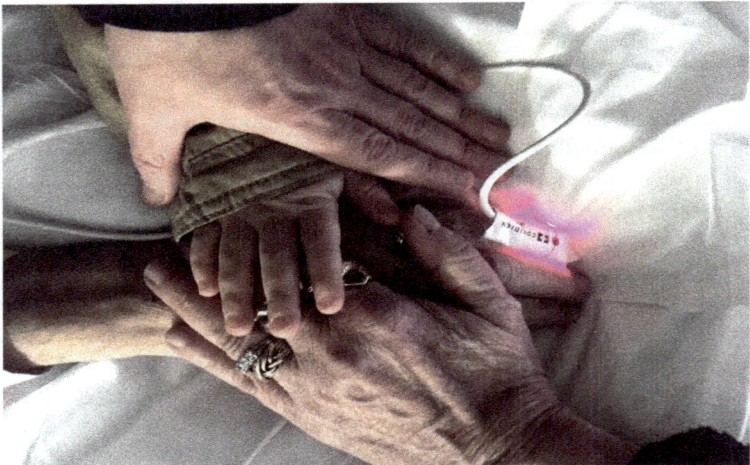

Figure 7. *Three Generations Holding Hands*, December 31, 2018.
Photograph by Krystal Demaine.

Attachment and Connection

From the moment humans are born, they look for a connection. Connection requires vulnerability but in return allows us to be present with other people on an unspoken level. When we are in a safe space where we can be vulnerable, like in therapy, we can find ways to connect to one another, to find comfort in emoting, expressing, communicating, and supporting as ways to find a connection. For my father and me, there was an unspoken way in which we bonded over music. Our connection did not involve words. It involved playing jazz, improvising, listening, and tuning in. All we had to do was pick up our instruments and begin to read a chart, and we knew just how to improvise the music together. There is a natural emotional yielding that occurs when playing music with others. Creating the musical aesthetic becomes intuitive through the connection of the people playing music together.

According to Stephen Porges (2011) polyvagal theory, the vagus nerve, which is responsible for emotional regulation and autonomic response, plays an important role in our attachment to others. The vagus nerve is the longest nerve in the human body. It runs from the start of the spinal cord in the brain, all the way through the lungs and heart, and down to the gut. The vagus nerve helps to regulate the autonomic nervous system, which controls bodily functions such as heart rate, respiration, sneezing, and swallowing. Importantly, it also interfaces with the sympathetic nervous system, to bring salve to the overstressed lungs, heart, and digestive tract. Stress on the other hand reduces vagus nerve activity. Things like swallowing, steady breathing, and a calm body gives me a sense, as a therapist that there is good vagal activity. When it comes to attachment, it is the vagus nerve that stimulates the parasympathetic nervous response when we feel safe and connected to others. This explains why when we feel fear or anxiety in situations, we feel a flutter of emotion in our head (headache), lungs (changes in respiration), gut (stomach pains), and heart (heartache).

Many of the relaxation techniques presented in this book can stimulate the vagus nerve. Singing and breathing, relaxing with music, drawing, and creating—all are great tools for tapping into the parasympathetic, stimulating the vagus nerve, reducing anxiety, and promoting greater mind and body connection. Porges (2011) postulates that attachment to others even increases vagal output. A sense of attachment promotes safety, wellness, and security and, in turn, helps to cultivate more ease in tapping the parasympathetic. With secure attachment during childhood, we have a better chance for self-regulation as adults.

Along similar lines, professor of psychiatry Dan Siegel (2012), in his research on his concept of interpersonal neurobiology, posits that the brain and mind are shaped by how we form our relationships with one another. That is, when we are emotionally connected to other people the chemicals that are released by those feelings of connection change how we think and operate. Interpersonal neurobiology is founded on the notion that the brain continues to change, grow, and develop throughout our lives, including after physical or psychological trauma. Therefore, when traumatic relationships have changed a person's brain, interpersonal neurobiology helps to build positive and healthy interpersonal relationships, doing so through the use of mindfulness-based practices.

Krystal L. Demaine

Being deeply loved by someone gives you strength, while loving someone deeply gives you courage.

—Laozi

Welcoming Loving Relationships

It is essential to human well-being to find a sense of belongingness and connection. When it comes to our emotional health, loving and caring relationships improve mood, happiness, and health. This is the biggest takeaway of the Harvard Study of Adult Development, the longest longitudinal study on adult health, whose fourth and current director is Robert Waldinger, a professor of clinical professor at Harvard Medical School (Waldinger, 2015). By studying the lives of 724 men over 80 years, this study has found that those who were the happiest, healthiest, and lived the longest were those who had healthy, bonded relationships. Those relationships may be with a sibling, partner, or friend. Regardless of the type of relationship, it led to more fulfilling lives for those people. Human connection makes us happy, which promotes our overall health. While our genes may give some indication of how healthy we will be, it is high-quality relationships that have been shown to bring greater wellness because they bring more meaning to life. When we lose our connection to others, perhaps through death or isolation, our mental health changes, negatively affecting not just the mind but the body's entire neurologic system, including both the central and peripheral nervous systems. Humans quite literally need each other to stay healthy and alive. Sometimes we don't feel that we belong unless we open ourselves up to belonging.

In the Torah, Adam is described originally as one, all, and androgynous. When Adam is split into two parts (posited as male and female), there arises a perpetual seeking of the union of the self again—the counterpart, the other half of the heart. The seeking is not sexual in nature—it is a search for deep intimacy with another, for entry into the heart of another to be whole. Rabbi Manis Friedman (2018), in *The Joy of Intimacy*, refers to this shared heart as a sacred space and suggests that we must see that shared space as a privilege. We need to respect the sacredness of each other's hearts and honor the vulnerability and authenticity needed to cultivate the intimacy for a strong relationship.

Love is powerful and has the capacity to heal. It has the will to bring us back to our original state of true compassion, and to the child within. When we forgot how to love ourselves or others, we learn how to reintegrate the value of belonging and love into our life.

Showing appreciation, respect, and gratitude for others can help grow our loving hearts and share the love with others.

Ancestral Cords

When we consider the roots of our behaviors, thoughts, emotions, and relationships, including the people we are drawn to, we may look to the invisible lines of connections; and sometimes those connections may be to our ancestors. In *Healing Ancestral Karma*, psychotherapist and shamanic healer Steven Farmer (2014) states that an ancestral connection can be a felt sense, not just a biological inheritance of DNA. Ancestral cords are the unseen threads of energy that bind our lineage. We can cognitively and behaviorally cut those cords by physically distancing ourselves from relationships that do not work for us. Yet even we separate our lives, a piece of the connection may continue to tag along. In her children's book *The Invisible String*, Patrice Karst (2000) illustrates the theme of invisible connection. Through the concept of heartstrings, Karst explains the connection we can feel to others even when a person is faraway or dies. One of the most vital lessons to share with a child is that no matter the distance, we can always feel connected to and loved by the people we care for.

Here is an illustration. Imagine a circle of people. One person takes a ball of yarn and wraps the end around their wrist a couple of times so that the yarn is attached to their body. Without letting go of the string, that person tosses the ball of yarn to another person, who does the same, looping the yarn around their wrist, then tossing the ball to yet another person. The ball of yarn is passed around the circle until everyone in the group has interacted with the yarn. What results is an interconnected web of yarn binding the group together; by design, everyone becomes connected to another person and each other. When one person sways or tugs at the yarn, the rest of the group can feel the movement. If someone lifts their arms, the movement is transferred like a wave to people on the other side of the circle. Now imagine the group is given a pair of scissors, and everyone is asked to cut themselves free from the interconnected web. People cut the threads on each side of their wrist, and the connecting threads crisscrossing through the middle of the circle fall to the floor. The web of yarn that kept everyone tethered and connected in movement and feeling has been severed. Yet even when the connection is cut, the visceral feeling of the connection the group once shared remains. And there is a wrap of yarn around each person's wrist that they take with them, even after they are disconnected. The illustration helps us see that we are connected, but freedom of movement is important, and if we want to build that connection again, we can reconnect that cord.

Research has shown that ancestral thread is carried in our DNA and can become ingrained in how we raise our children, how we react to situations, and how we make decisions. When I was pregnant with my son, I read an article published in the *Journal of Spiritual Mental Health* that pointed to guilt as being part of the Jewish legacy. There was a joke at the top of the article that wrote, "What is Jewish Alzheimer's disease? It is when you forget everything but the guilt" (Dein, 2013, p. 123). The article highlights the stereotype of intrinsic guilt and anxiety among Ashkenazi Jews, who may carry an abundance of intergenerational trauma.

The field of epigenetics studies inherited trauma, also referred to as intergenerational trauma, sometimes called transgenerational trauma. The term intergenerational trauma was introduced in the 1940s by Conrad Waddington, a British embryologist. Epigenetics understands our DNA to contain memories and imprints of our ancestors, which flows in the blood through the thousands of miles of arteries and veins. What we inherit are the emotions related to the traumas, which can cause changes in the DNA: my mother's experience of trauma transforms her DNA so that I, as her child, also carry that trauma (Deichmann, 2016). On a societal level, the deep trauma from colonization, holocaust, genocide, and enslavement affects specific groups of people. In his groundbreaking book *My Grandmother's Hands* (2017), Resmaa Menakem discusses how Africans were forcibly brought to the Americas and enslaved and how this built anxiety and shame that became embedded in the body and passed along to their descendants. This trauma has been reinforced through political policy and institutions that lack understanding or compassion for this legacy. Racist and prejudiced speech and actions from world leaders only enforce destructive behaviors that trickle down the generations and maintain the trauma cycle.

In 2018, a study published in the *Proceedings of the National Academy of Sciences of the United States* (Costa et al., 2018) found evidence of intergenerational trauma in sons of US Civil War soldiers who had been held as prisoners of war, including in sons born after the war, who were not exposed to the horrific traumas that their fathers had experienced. It was found that even sons with no direct exposure to war lived more stressful and even shorter lives than their fathers, perhaps indicating that the stresses of war were passed down to the next generation. Research in the field of intergenerational trauma is quite young, and most of the research has been on Holocaust survivors.

Researchers Rachel Yehuda and Amy Lehrner examined longitudinal studies of large groups and found that descendants of Holocaust survivors had higher levels of stress hormones, suggesting intergenerational transmission of anxiety (Yehuda & Lehrner, 2018).

Our long line of ancestors carries many stories. We are cognizant of some, but others are unknown, perhaps becoming lost in the lineage. These stories and all of the emotions associated with them become imprinted in our bloodlines and nestled in the rhythm of our heart vibration. Like a tree of life, we are rooted in an ancient system that interconnects us to a vast community of ancestors. Current DNA testing kits can allow us to see a glimmer of our relationships with the past and can be easily ordered online. It can be interesting to see the lineage that makes us.

The Lives We Never Knew

Sometimes the ancestors that we never knew can cause us the most grief. We can spend time examining our childhoods and the experiences, losses, and grievances to make sense of our own stories. Sometimes we imagine what life could have been if that person had been in our lives or had been in our lives with in a different capacity.

Historian Ellen Herman (2008), in her book *Kinship by Design*, discusses how the early 1970s, a time when abortion was illegal in the United States, saw a spike in unwed pregnancies, which resulted in mothers relinquishing their babies to adoption agencies. In 1973, the Supreme Court ruled abortion a legal practice across the United States. This ruling was overturned in 2022, but families continue to choose not to birth children for any number of reasons.

Mark Evans and colleagues (2014) reviewed the literature on selective reduction, a method that began in the 1980s when pregnant women who utilized fertility treatment found themselves with unsought multiple fetuses. To reduce the risks related to giving birth to multiple babies, pregnant women could select a fetal reduction. Although fetal reduction involves an explicitly conscious decision, complicated grief is prevalent among women after such perinatal loss. According to Anette Kersting and Birgit Wagner (2012), trauma related to prenatal loss, especially without therapeutic support, can lead to PTSD. Pregnancy loss, whether from stillbirth, fetal reduction, miscarriage, or another cause, is a traumatic life event, and therefore it is important to recognize the lives that could have been.

Leading clinical therapist in family-inherited trauma Mark Wolynn (2016) highlights riveting stories of ancestral trauma in his book

It Didn't Start with You. Wolynn discusses the case of Jesse, a 20-year-old college athlete, who spiraled into a deep depression and dropped out of college because of bouts of extreme anxiety that manifested as body chills, insomnia, and a sense of impending doom. Jesse came to see Wolynn after unsuccessfully consulting with many medical and mental health professionals. Wolynn recalls that even though Jesse was only 20 years old, he looked a decade older. After hearing Jesse describe his symptoms, Wolynn asked if there was a history of significant family trauma that might have involved being cold while sleeping. Jesse revealed that he had only just recently found out that an uncle, whom he had never met, had frozen to death while working on power lines in a severe snowstorm, some 30 years earlier. Because of the pain of the tragic death, the family did not mention the story until Jesse's twentieth birthday, after which he began experiencing his symptoms. Working with Wolynn, Jesse connected his chills and insomnia with the unconscious terror of falling asleep, developed after hearing how his uncle had died. Making this connection allowed Jesse to separate his own identity from his uncle's and in turn build a healthier connection to his family member he had not previously known.

Etty Hillesum was a Jewish writer who became known to the world when her diaries were published posthumously. Hillesum was killed at Auschwitz concentration camp in 1943 when she was only 29 years old. On September 15, 1942, at 10:30 a.m., Hillesum wrote, "To think that one small heart can experience so much, oh God, so much suffering and so much love, I am so grateful to you, God, for having chosen my heart, in these times, to experience all the things it has experienced. The heart can't know the love without the pain" (Hillesum & Smelik, 2002, p. 514). Despite the horrors Hillesum faced, she was able to find beauty and meaning in her young life. This has given inspiration to those of us who face difficulties, aversion, and the unexpected stories that life challenges us with.

Whether the lives of our ancestors were never lived or never known, if we so choose, we hold a place in our hearts for those ancestors. We can still feel them connected to our heart and sometimes sense them tugging at our heartstrings. Our senses and our nerves have instincts that extend deep into our ancestors' experiences and are passed down into our own nervous systems; we can tune into those instinctual ancestral frequencies. Rituals of practice for recognizing those that were lost or those that never lived can aid in healing, connection, and understanding.

Trauma in the Brain and Body

Trauma leaves an impact on the mind, brain, and body. These changes in response to the traumatic experience are always close at hand. Memories of the trauma may keep coming up in our minds. When it comes to the brain, the neurologic changes caused by traumatic experiences can lead to things like memory loss, increased stress, anxiety, and depression. Trauma keeps the body in a hypervigilant state as a way of protecting the body from anticipated danger. When we experience PTSD, we can become stuck in hypervigilance, which floods the body with stress hormones and in turn reduces immune function (Uddin et al., 2010).

Our minds have a way of playing and replaying past experiences like scenes from a movie. Flashbacks involve a scene in our minds that take us back to an event in time. When these reexperienced scenes involve trauma, they are known as flashbacks. According to trauma expert Bessel van der Kolk (2014), neuroimaging has shown that traumatic flashbacks cause small lesions or traumas to the brain. These lesions are similar to those that occur with head traumas, such as a stroke, which in effect causes brain damage by hemorrhage. With a flashback, however, the damage is on a much smaller scale. These brain traumas or lesions appear on a brain scan as a blacked-out area of damaged brain cells, which are no longer receiving blood flow and therefore die. Trauma affects the mental flexibility of imagination—the brain finds it difficult to create new ideas and thought patterns. In other words, when we experience a flashback, it is almost as if the brain is experiencing the first-hand trauma again. And it can be unpredictable when a flashback will occur and for how long it will last. The cyclical loop of trauma is interrupted only with the right kind of treatment. The body needs to learn that the danger of the traumatic experience has passed and that we can live in the reality of the present. It is not an easy thing to live in the present reality if the body is stuck in a sympathetic hypervigilant state.

Just like physical trauma, traumatic emotional experiences and stress, as a result of the increased cortisol and inflammation, can cause an everlasting change in the brain's ability to manage stress. The fear centers in the brain become overactive and other areas of the brain become neglected and underused, with lower function and activity. When trauma or fearful experiences occur and the body goes into fight-or-flight mode, the capacity to formulate language can be reduced. Specifically, the amygdala, a structure in the midbrain responsible for emotions, becomes hyperactive and, in turn, verbal communication about the traumatic experience becomes inhibited and inaccessible.

Fortunately, we are able to retrain the brain to respond differently to those traumatic memories. Music, art, and creative movement are wonderful nonverbal means of expression, which can allow the mind to communicate what the body feels.

One of van der Kolk's (2014) most well-known findings is that our bodies hold trauma and pain arising from trauma and stress. This stress compromises the immune system and makes us more susceptible to depression, weight gain, fatigue, and sleeplessness. When a woman is pregnant and trauma occurs during her pregnancy, the chemicals produced during the trauma change the baby's DNA and nervous system. Clinical relationship experts, Dr's John and Julie Gottman, founders of the Gottman Method, observed and coded the emotional interactions of parents during their last trimester of pregnancy. The emotional interactions predicted for a 3-month-old infant, the vagal tone, the amount of laughter, crying, and positive affect, and the infant's ability to be soothed. This shows that stress affects the intra-uterine environment for the developing fetus and predicts the infant's ability to self-regulate. In response to their research, the Gottman Institute developed a 2-day workshop called, "Bringing Baby Home" designed for health care providers who support pregnant and parenting couples for a successful transition to parenthood (Gottman & Gottman, 2008).

The more trauma we experience in our lives, the more dissociated we are from our bodies. Our life stories inform how we live and connect with ourselves and others as well as with our bodies as well as our mind and heart. This is why it is important to work with our whole bodies for healing, not just the psyche. Van der Kolk suggests that activities engaging the mind and body, like yoga, can help rewire a brain that, because of trauma, has become stuck, perhaps in the sympathetic nervous system response. Wiring developed in childhood can be changed through bottom up (whole-body integration) approaches like drama therapy, music therapy, and psychodramas. Using these methods, we can enact what we have previously experienced and observe those lived stories in a safe and therapeutic environment.

When we ignore the past, it can come back to haunt us. The unseen personal and family histories of trauma that we hold in our bodies need to be heard—even if our conscious mind does not allow us to yet share those stories. Perhaps, as in the case of Jesse, we need the right entry point for those stories to emerge from the subconscious. Working through trauma takes vulnerability and courage, and working with the heart is one of the most important things we can do to heal trauma. Our pain is buoyant—even if we push it down, it will eventually pop back up. If we are brave enough to create an opportunity to examine how we feel and sail through the rough waters of those thoughts, feelings, and emotions, we can heal ourselves and make a change for our wellness and that of generations to come.

Creating Our Story

Civil rights activist and novelist James Baldwin affirmed that we are not born with our stories and our identities but that they are something that we develop. No one knows our story better than we do; we must therefore assert ourselves in the world (Meade and Baldwin, 1971).

As a shy and quiet child, I did not know how to assert myself, and when things bothered me, I never outwardly expressed my concerns, particularly in front of strangers. When I went to summer camp, the counselors began to notice my lack of assertiveness. During one Sunday campfire, each of the campers was asked to write a thematic poem. The theme my counselors assigned to me was "assertive." I did not know what the word meant, so I guessed its meaning; and I was able to write my poem and began to understand the reason my counselors asked me to explore the topic.

My great-grandparents were members of a Latvian tribe that has come to be synonymous with poverty in Latvia and Lithuania as the result of a legacy of trauma. Latvia, known as Courland when my family lived there, has a long history of political violence, war, and oppression. In the mid- to late 1800s when the violence became unbearable in Latvia, families like mine set out to plant new roots in a new place.

When I was building my career in music therapy, I would speak to my father about my challenges and worries. He would often respond by telling me to be strong and to let those concerns go, that the stress of the issue would cause me more harm than good. I took on a lot of stress in my relationships with others and neglected the all-important assertive awareness that I needed to communicate my story and my feelings. There is great importance in standing up for oneself to make a change. In addition, work hard, do not complain, and keep your chin up—this has been a code in my family and something that has been a mantra that my parents passed down to me.

Thich Nhat Hanh (2013) explains that, although we often inherit a legacy of suffering, we also have the potential to transform it:

> When we're still young, many of us are determined to be different from our parents. We say we'll never make our children suffer. But when we grow up, we tend to behave just

like our parents, and we make others suffer because, like our ancestors, we don't know how to handle the energies we've inherited. We've received many positive and negative seeds from our parents and ancestors. They transmitted their habit to us because they didn't know how to transform it. (p. 6)

Along similar lines, Louise Hay (1999) suggests in her Power Thought Cards that our love can liberate our legacy from suffering: "I have compassion for my parents' childhoods. I now know that I chose them because they were perfect for what I had to learn. I forgive them and set them free, and I set myself free. I see my parents as tiny children who need love." Knowing how our ancestors (parents) lived, can give us an opportunity for compassion for their suffering.

Within our hearts, we hold our ancestors' traumas, hopes, and dreams. Their suffering and gifts can become our suffering and gifts. How can we give gratitude to our ancestors, recognizing that we would not be here without them? No matter how you have understood your heritage, whether there has been neglect, conflict, trauma, or love, we need to acknowledge that we all have received the seeds of suffering. When we can recognize our suffering and the suffering of our ancestors, we can begin to heal by exploring the stories and how those stories relate to our identity—the stories that we create for our lives.

Companion Listening #8

"Grandma's Hands" by Bill Withers (1971)

Creative Exercise #8: Lines in the Hand

Imagine the blood pumping through the veins of all humans, carrying the DNA of hundreds of thousands of years of ancestors. Their existence can be found in the hand, the roots, and lines that we can see, our life, our being. Take a moment to look at your hand. You may look with your eyes and feel the line textures with your fingertips. Focus on the details of the hand. Consider what your hands do and the contributions they have made to your life.

Using art supplies, create a print of your hand. Some ways to do this:
- Sketch your hand on paper.
- Pour paint on your palm and press your painted palm onto paper.
- Use clay to make an imprint of your hand.
- Take a photograph of your hand.
- Cover your hand in plaster and create a cast of your hand.
- Create more prints of the hands of your family members.

Once you have created your handprint, begin to make an objective list of what you see related to the color or colors, shape, form, lines, the number of lines, depth and length of lines, ridges, symbols, cross lines, long lines, the shape of the finger, fingernails, fingernail beds, bitten nails, cuticles, knuckles, and skin quality (dry, course, cracked, smooth, soft, wounded, scratched, cut).

Once you have made your list, begin completing phrases about the hand:

My hand feels . . . My hand sees . . . My hand holds . . . My hand touches . . . My hand knows . . . My hand looks . . . My hand carries . . . My hand tickles . . . My hand senses . . . My hand emerges from . . . My hand clasps . . . My hand captures . . . My hand soothes . . . My hand eases . . . My hand hears . . . My hand remembers . . . My hand knows . . . My hand wonders . . . My hand contains . . .

Once you have completed your phrases, choose one as a starting point and continue building from it. Turn that phrase into a story, more phrases, a poem, or even a song. Perhaps the phrase will evolve to discuss where your hand goes, what it does, its history, and its connections. Perhaps the hand will connect to another hand, and the story will emerge with two or more hands. See where your story of the hand takes you and how this helps connect to your identity, your ancestors, your life, and your relationships with others.

References

Costa, D. L., Yetter, N., & DeSomer, H. (2018). Intergenerational transmission of paternal trauma among US Civil War ex-POWs. *Proceedings of the National Academy of Sciences of the United States of America, 115*(44), 11215–11220. https://doi.org//10.1073/pnas.1803630115

Deichmann, U. (2016). Epigenetics: The origins and evolution of a fashionable topic. *Developmental Biology, 416*(1), 249–254.

Dein, S. (2013). The origins of Jewish guilt: Psychological, theological, and cultural perspectives. *Journal of Spirituality in Mental Health, 15*(2), 123–137. https://doi.org//10.1080/19349637.2012.737682

Evans, M., Andriole, S., & Britt, D. (2014). Fetal reduction: 25 years' experience. *Fetal Diagnosis and Therapy, 4*(35), 69–82

Farmer, S. (2014). *Healing ancestral karma: Free yourself from unhealthy family patterns.* Hierophant Publishing.

Friedman, M. (2018). *The joy of intimacy: A soulful guide to keeping the spark alive.* It's Good to Know Publishing.

Gottman, J. M., & Gottman, J. S. (2008). *And baby makes three: The six-step plan for preserving marital intimacy and rethinking romance after baby arrives.* Three Rivers Press.

Hanh, T. N. (2006). *Present moment wonderful moment.* Parallax Press.

Hanh, T. N. (2013). *The art of communicating.* HarperCollins.

Hay, L. (1999). Power thought cards [Card game]. Hay House.

Herman, E. (2008). *Kinship by design: A history of adoption in the modern United States.* University of Chicago Press.

Hillesum, E., & Smelik, K. (2002). *Etty: The letters and diaries of Etty Hillesum, 1941–1943.* Eerdmans Publishing Company.

Karst, P. (2000). *The invisible string.* DeVorss & Co.

Kersting, A., & Wagner, B. (2012). Complicated grief after perinatal loss. *Dialogues in Clinical Neuroscience, 14*(2), 187–194.

Meade, M., & Baldwin, J. (1971). *A rap on race.* Michael Joseph.

Menakem, R. (2017). *My grandmother's hands: Racialized trauma and the pathway to mending our hearts and bodies.* Central Recover Press.

Porges, S. W. (2011). *The polyvagal theory: Neurophysiological foundations of emotions, attachment, communication, and self-regulation.* W. W. Norton and Co.

Siegel, D. (2012). *Pocket guide to interpersonal neurobiology: An integrative handbook of the mind.* W. W. Norton.

Uddin, M., Aiello, A. E., Wildman, D. E., Koenen, K. C., Pawelec, G., de Los Santos, R., Goldmann, E., & Galea, S. (2010). Epigenetic and immune function profiles associated with posttraumatic stress disorder. *Proceedings of the National Academy of Sciences of the United States of America, 107*(20), 9470–9475. https://doi.org/10.1073/pnas.0910794107

van der Kolk, B. (2014). *The body keeps the score: Brain, mind, and body in the healing of trauma.* Penguin Books.

Waldinger, R. (2015). *What makes a good life? Lessons from the longest study on happiness* [Video]. TED Conferences. https://www.ted.com/talks/robert_waldinger_what_makes_a_good_life_lessons_from_the_longest_study_on_happiness

Wolynn, M. (2016). *It didn't start with you: How inherited family trauma shapes who you are and how to end the cycle.* Random House.

Woodward, S. (2019). Fetal, neonatal, and early infant experiences of maternal singing. In D. Howard, J. Nix, & G. Welch (Eds.), *The Oxford handbook of singing* (pp. 431–453). Oxford University Press.

Yehuda, R., & Lehrner, A. (2018). Intergenerational transmission of trauma effects: Putative role of epigenetic mechanisms. *World Psychiatry, 17*(3), 243–257.

Chapter 9

Healing the Ancestral Heart

I walked a mile with Pleasure; she chatted all the way;
But left me none the wiser for all she had to say.
I walked a mile with Sorrow; and ne'er a word said she;
But, oh! The things I learned from her, when Sorrow walked with me.
—Robert Browning Hamilton, *Along the Road*

Dark Crystals

In Jim Henson and Frank Oz's 1982 fantasy adventure film *The Dark Crystal*, a large, magical crystal that represents the truth is the key to bringing balance to the mystical world of Thra. Importantly, the crystal brings together a powerful species of creature, which splits into two when a shard of the crystal breaks off—thus turning the crystal dark. The split creates two groups: the Mystics and the Skeksis, the good and the evil. Even with the crystal broken, the two groups continue to be intrinsically linked; when one Mystic dies, their Skeksis counterpart also dies. The antagonist Skeksis seeks to take control over the crystal and gain immortality and more power.

While Henson and Oz's film may give a sense of the power and the relationship between good and evil, it also serves as a reminder of the important things in life and the balance in maintaining the health of those elements. In our lives, we can stumble upon sacred and vital experiences that bring us joy and meaning, something that I call the precious gemstones of life. Giving birth to a child, completing a degree, getting a job, or healing from an illness—overcoming such great feats and finding peace at the end of it all gives our experiences special meaning. Sometimes those events that are beautiful may be clouded or muddled, even shrouded in mystery, like the dark crystal. These perplexing experiences persuade us to sit and ponder their mysteries to find clarity or meaning. The ancestral heart is deeply rooted in family history and may hold trauma or fears that can lie dormant in unconscious energy, while new rhythmic vibrations are carried in the blood. Like the dark crystal, the precious gemstones of life may carry hidden messages that can help us heal.

115

In the wellness world, supported by discoveries in the field of quantum physics, crystals have been thought to have healing properties or a spiritual effect, with each crystal possessing a unique vibrational frequency. In the West, pink Himalayan salt rocks are sold in many stores, and people even grind the rock and cook food with its tiny crystals. Just before my father died, and when I was seeking help for body inflammation and headaches, I did a treatment session in polarity therapy, a form of energy medicine. According to the American Polarity Therapy Association (2021), polarity therapy has been found to improve circulation, inflammation, and stress and to promote overall energy and balance in the body. During the treatment session, I lay prone, covered with thickly layered blankets, on a heated massage table in a dark room. I closed my eyes as the practitioner placed various crystals and stones on my body to send polarized energy to the subtle body just above my physical body's surface, the liminal part of the body that is neither physical nor spiritual. Like traditional Chinese medicine and other forms of energetic bodywork (e.g., reflexology, yoga, and craniosacral therapy), polarity therapy works to restore movement and balance by stimulating the body's energy, known as qi in traditional Chinese medicine and as prana in yoga. During the session, I could feel the stones being placed on my body and I could feel the practitioner's hands lying still and then moving to a part of my back. I understood that moving her hands was a method of balancing the polarity of the energy being emitted by the crystals. At the end of the session, I sat up and the practitioner told me her assessment, that I was generally quite energetically balanced. We talked about holding energy in the body and maintaining energetic balance through activities such as mediation, yoga, playing music, and other forms of relaxation. I felt deeply calmed by the entire experience and left feeling curious to learn more about the vibrations and properties of different crystals.

The dark crystal is a clear gem crystal with a cloudy color that is said to promote serenity and calm. Crystals can grow in almost any place on the Earth, forming geodes and prisms from molecules that become electrically charged to form repeating layers and shapes. There may be a scientific basis for the soothing effect created by energy balancing with crystals; the placebo effect may contribute to crystals' healing power as well. As a young girl, I was fascinated by crystals and gemstones. I had a collection of stones, which I cherished and kept in tiny boxes in my bedroom. I frequently went to shops to buy semiprecious stones, and I kept a log of the stones I collected. I researched their origin, colors, and composition through books at the library.

The memories, thoughts, and residual emotions in our life take shape and harden over time, like crystals. Each pattern is unique, but each continues to replicate, becoming perhaps unexpectedly large or beautiful or sharp. Sometimes we feel that we are so clear about what we are doing, that we have it all mapped out, and sometimes life can become murky, complicated, or difficult to understand. When things do not turn out the way we want, we can tend to split our emotions and our psychological wellness can take two different paths. Without the dark, we cannot know the light. As Thich Nhat Hanh's (2014) book *No Mud, No Lotus* shows, we cannot know happiness without suffering. The dark can bring us to unexpected places that can yield magical outcomes for the greater good. We need to first recognize the precious gemstones in life, value them, and accept that they may become broken or shattered, that we may need to work to overcome challenges and find repair. The key to facing challenges is being patient, striving for the best outcome, and working hard. We need to sit and listen to the metaphorical dark crystals in our life; we need to take time to process and understand what is being communicated to us through the hidden messages. Whether we use the crystal as a metaphor for a child, a partner, a coworker, or an unseen family member, it is important to take the time to find clarity and seek the truth.

Honor Our Ancestors

Each morning when I wake up, I say a prayer for my father. Each night before I go to bed, I do the same. I say that I am so grateful for all that I have today and so sad for all the things that I cannot hold and touch anymore. On anniversary mornings, I light a candle and burn incense at the home altar that I built for my father. I allow the aroma of the incense to remind me through my olfactory sense that I am alive and that I am grateful for each day. I stretch and practice yoga, write, drink tea, and play my electric guitar using my dad's amplifier. The amp is my electrical connection to Dad, and it is one way that we now communicate.

The way I honor my father is uniquely mine. There is no one way to honor the death of a loved one. Honoring the loss can be a therapeutic process to bridge a connection between the living and the dead, or it can be a one-time acknowledgment to say goodbye. In some cultures, there is an annual day to celebrate the lives of those who once lived. Many Latin American cultures celebrate the Day of the Dead, or Día de Los Muertos, with parades, festivities, and decorations to honor the departed. Many Christians celebrate All Souls' Day as a day of prayer and remembrance for those who have passed. People of the Catholic faith celebrate All Saints' Day, observed by leaving offerings on graves and attending church services. In some cultures, there is a belief that if we ignore our ancestors after death, we will receive bad luck or bad karma (Farmer, 2014).

Figure 8. *Ancestral Papers, IV*, 2019. Mixed media (acrylic, gold leaf, India ink) on paper, 7 x 4 in. Artist: Constance Vallis. Reproduced by permission from Constance Vallis.

In Chinese culture, the loss of loved ones is honored in many ways, from Tomb Sweeping Day to the Hungry Ghost Festival. Throughout China, there are spiritual temples, and on any day, someone can walk in and burn incense to honor the people who have died. Some of the temples that I have visited in China have burning areas both inside and outside the buildings, or incense burners hung from ceilings, on walls, and in burning bowls on the floor. Small altars can also be found throughout the streets and in restaurants, with offerings such as fruit and other small gifts for the person who has died.

In many Chinese, Daoist, and Buddhist traditions, honoring the dead involves the burning of joss papers, also known as ancestral papers, Chinese papers, or ghost papers. These papers are traditionally made of thin bamboo or rice paper and are decorated with stamps or specific seals related to a deity. Sometimes the papers are decorated to look like money, to be offered to the dead when burned. For the past forty years, printmaker and painter Constance Vallis has embedded joss papers into her artwork (shown above). The joss papers in her series are layered with silver or gold leaf on mulberry or bamboo paper. She usually places a swash of ink on the paper and lays the leaf on top, sometimes stamping the work with her etchings.

Constance grew up in the Greek Orthodox tradition, and everything in her church was gilded, with rich and dense color. She felt called to work with the joss papers because of the spiritual aspect and the lightness that the paper brought to her artwork. Creating art that feels light gives a sense of clarity and helps her connect to her ancestral roots. She said, "Many Americans are disconnected from their ancestors, and regardless of the relationship, even after death, our ancestors can give us a powerful line of understanding of where we've been that connects us to where we are going" (C. Vallis, personal communication, July 20, 2020).

The psychotherapist and healer Steven Farmer (2014) claims we have three types of ancestors, spiritual ancestors, biological ancestors, and territorial ancestors. Our biological ancestors are those with a DNA connection to us, our parents and grandparents. Territorial ancestors are those that once lived on the land where we currently live. We show respect for our territorial ancestors by honoring the traditions of the people from that land and by respecting the land and the culture of that area. Spiritual ancestors are those that once walked on the earth and to whom we feel a spiritual or cultural connection, even if they are not part of our blood lineage.

Expectations

In listening to music, we can anticipate what will come next in the melody, a concept known as musical expectation. For example, if we sing the ascending Western diatonic scale, do-re-mi-fa-sol-la-ti, we expect the melody to resolve back to do. If we are left hanging in ti, we can begin to feel emotionally unsettled and potentially aggravated. David Huron (2007) writes about the subject in his book *Sweet Anticipation*, which is based on his studies of music stimulating emotions, laughter, and chills. When we listen to familiar music, we can anticipate the climax and how it will prompt us to sing, make us feel, hold us, and comfort us. Musical expectation is one of the most wonderful and exciting parts of music. In our everyday lives, we build expectations of how things will be, how we will go about our plans for the day, how our food will taste, and how our partners or coworkers will react to certain situations. But life throws us surprises, and we need to be prepared to improvise. We need to be prepared for the unexpected.

In *Far from the Tree: Parents, Children, and the Search for Identity*, Andrew Solomon (2012) discuss how we do not always meet expectations, especially of our parents. Parents plant a seed of their selves in a child and believe the child will mirror them. When the child does meet this expectation and is furthermore born with a neurological condition or a mental health challenge that is not shared by the parent(s), these differences become the child's identity. We do not always grow into the trees that our parents intended to seed. This includes children conceived out of rape or those that become criminals, transgender, or are prodigies. Perhaps the child is drawing on a deep-rooted sense of identity in the bloodline, unseen or not yet tapped.

In Kahlil Gibran's (1923/1951), *The Prophet*, the people of the village of Orphalese listen to a wise prophet, who expounds on various topics from the top of a hill. One person asks him to speak about children, and the prophet says:

> Your children are not your children. They are the sons and daughters of Life's longing for itself. They come through you but not from you, and though they are with you, yet they belong not to you. You may give them your love but not your thoughts, for they have their own thoughts. You may house their bodies but not their souls, for their souls dwell in the house of tomorrow, which you cannot visit, not in your dreams. You may strive to be like them, but seek not to make them like you. For life goes not backward nor tarries with yesterday. (p. 17)

We are all children of the universe brought here to continue the journey of life. Sometimes parents' expectations of their children are cultivated by the environment, rather than the parent alone or by what precedes in the family lineage. Sara shared with me the story of her closed adoption, without access to her original birth certificate, her birth mother's name or identity, or any other birth information. As a baby, Sara lived with a foster care family until six weeks old, when she was adopted through a Jewish adoption agency in Virginia. From as early as she can remember, she knew she was adopted. Now as a 40-year-old woman, Sara has a strong desire to connect with her biological roots and to investigate her ancestry, bloodline, and DNA, which has always seemed a mysterious void in her life. After completing a DNA test, she discovered that her ancestors came from a host of countries, which did not give her any insight into her roots.

A few years before she decided to become a mother herself, Sara began to experience physical pain. Pain that had been somewhat in the background and compartmentalized for most of her life began to surface. She began to think that her first child would be the first biological relative that she knew. Thinking about the ramifications of starting a family brought up many thoughts and feelings for Sara. One thought was of not being a good enough mother. She had a primal wound related to being given away for adoption and wondered why her biological mother did not keep her. On an intellectual level, Sara thought perhaps it was not feasible for her mother to keep her, perhaps her mother was too young, or maybe she was sick. These thoughts and questions became recurring themes for years. Over time, Sara began to feel guilty for these thoughts, which were causing her so much anxiety. She thought, "I should feel grateful that I was adopted." Yet she continued to question whether she was unmourned, unacknowledged, or lost.

When an adoptee is cut off from their biological lineage, society does not often acknowledge it as a real loss, unlike in a death, which is a more socially condoned loss. Sara began living in an in-between realm, one foot in and one foot out; she felt like she was splitting into two. She recognized that, in a way, she did meet her biological mother when she was inside of her womb, even though she does not remember that relationship. When Sara began to create altered books (an artistic process of transforming books to modify their appearance), she was able to find a way to metaphorically search for her biological mother. Her exploration of attachment came clear to her as she altered words and images in ways that symbolized being in the limbo

121

of time and space, floating in the water, and examining the parts of herself that were unborn. Even though her art making was characterized by painful loss, she also had a sense of finding herself on a blank canvas. Even if she did not know where she came from, what her story was, or what place to put herself in, she found it both liberating and sad to be able to walk through different worlds and create her roots through writing, including poems and short stories, and through art.

In *The Soul's Code* (1996), psychologist James Hillman says that we are all looking to create our biography. A biography, not just from science, genetics, or our traumas but from our calling, our imagination, and what we want it to be. Though there may be genetic explanations for whom we feel we must be—the interplay of genetics and environment does not allow space for the feeling to be you, whatever being you is. We may question why siblings have different behaviors, thoughts, and emotions. Living a plot by genetic code, society, or our parents' expectations for who we are can only inhibit our true story, which centers around what we are meant to do and how we are meant to live. Hillman says we can create what we want our stories to be, and we have a calling to live those stories, an idea he proposes as the acorn theory. Hillman postulates that we are born with a character that has been given to us and not by our genetics or environment, although they may have some influence. He claims that our parents came together— an egg and sperm were preselected in the union—to create our birth into this world. Our parents came together not for personal unity, Hillman suggests, but to create us. According to the acorn theory, our behavior is preselected and passed on from our parents' existing behaviors. It also claims the child is called to these parents and that the parents need to help the child cultivate their calling as parents, which allows the child to live fully. Rejecting a child's abilities or not listening to a child's story can fuel the inner critic and lead to feelings of inferiority. It is during childhood that we need to develop the greatest connections and bonds and have our stories heard so that we can be more independent adults.

How do we allow for the unfolding of identity, especially when it comes to our children? I think self-listening, imagining, and creating can reveal who we are, what we need, and how we are going to obtain what we need. Hillman (1996) argues that children are living two lives, the one that they are called to live and the one that their environment or their parents want for them. Hillman believes that it is the environment that puts the child into dysfunction, causes mental health problems, and instills in them the idea that they are not doing what they need to do. In other words, limiting their independence, creativity, and calling leads to psychopathology. The psychoanalyst Alfred Adler argued a similar point, that the cultivation of the inferiority complex can lead to psychopathologies and neurosis when a child is told, either consciously or subconsciously, that they are less than what they were born to be (Hoffman, 2020).

Sometimes we can manifest inferiority because of an experience or an impression that has been cast on us. But if we look inward and begin to explore our deep narrative questioning, the source of our thoughts can help lead to understanding and release. The nurturing begins from within. After suffering adversity, depression, an eating disorder, addiction, and a marriage that she did not want to be a part of, author Byron Katie examined this suffering as a way to find joy. She developed a mindful practice of asking four questions and refers to these questions as "the work." Katie asks: (1) Is it true? (2) How can I absolutely know it is true? (3) How do you react when you believe your thought? and (4) Who would you be without the thought? (Katie & Mitchell, 2002, pp. 18–19). The relationship that we have with our thoughts, Katie says, is the most sacred and intimate relationship that we can have; and if we probe ourselves with four questions about our authentic truth, we will find the answers. We just need to listen to what is within.

Nurturing the Inner Child

We have the ability within ourselves to unlock and release harmful experiences to create healthy changes for our future. Experiences that we endure, oftentimes forgotten and sometimes inherited from previous generations, can be held deep within the inner child. Within each of us, there is an inner child that needs nurturing.

The inner child can be imagined as a physical representation of the self or as an imagined felt sense. Sprightly into the world the inner child is born, pure, creative, and free . . . Like an angel on the shoulder when we are in conflict, the inner child serves as the ever-present subconscious part of the self (Demaine, 2018, p. 151).

It is the inner child, as I see it, that is the self we can turn to for advice, and it is this inner child that we also need to protect. When the inner child is criticized or exposed to difficult, taboo, or inappropriate situations, the child can become a wounded bird, unable to soar through the sky or discouraged from doing so. Scenarios that impair the inner child serve as a source of fuel for the inner critic—the judging self (Demaine, 2018). The inner critic is fueled by inferiority. The inner child can be more forgiving.

Dr. Seuss's (1957) *How the Grinch Stole Christmas* tells the tale of a grumpy character who lives in the snowy mountains away from all of the other villagers in the quaint town of Whoville. The Grinch is said to have been born with a heart three sizes too small, which has made him extremely grumpy. On Christmas, the Grinch is so averse to the merriment that he burglarizes the homes of villagers, stealing all their holiday gifts and decorations. However, as a child, the Grinch had a warm and caring heart even when he was ridiculed by his peers as unacceptably different for his green hair and his unusual taste for moldy food. As an adult, the Grinch is forced outside of the village, which fuels his inner critic and causes his resentment and anger toward the villagers.

When parents offer their children empathy and help them to cope with negative feelings like anger, sadness, and fear, parents build bridges of loyalty and affection.
–John M. Gottman, *Raising an Emotionally Intelligent Child*

When unconditional love and regard are given to us, it permits us to be whom we need to be and to do what we need to do. Humanistic psychologist Abraham Maslow famously said, "A musician must make music, an artist must paint, a poet must write, if he is to be ultimately at peace with himself. What a man can be, he must be" (quoted in Carducci, 2009, p. 239). At the pinnacle of Maslow's hierarchy of needs is self-actualization (doing what one needs to do), which cannot be achieved until self-esteem, belongingness, safety, and physiological needs are met.

The inner child can be easily provoked by both internal and external forces. The stronger the compassion and understanding we receive, the greater resilience the inner child will have. Nurturing the inner child by engaging in childlike wonder through playing, art making, dancing, music making, or drawing closer to nature can spark the same sense of curiosity and wonder that originally cultivated the child within. We often say that we are growing *up* in the world, but if we look more closely, we may consider that we are deepening or rooting down as we become more grounded and closer to the authentic self within. We can develop a closer edge to self-actualization—of doing what we need to do, by finding an authentic way of being. Indian philosopher Jiddu Krishnamurti (1895–1986) famously said, "Observing without evaluating is the form of human intelligence." Krishnamurti's recognition of nonjudgment is the key to quieting the inner critic and nurturing the inner child. It is judgment that gives the critic its fuel. Let's show compassion for our children and our heart and show acceptance that it is all a journey to get closer to the roots of the Earth.

The Beams of Love

In the poem "The Little Black Boy," English printmaker and poet William Blake wrote, "We are here on Earth for a little space, that we may learn to endure the beams of love" (1789/2021, p. 10, para. 4). We are willing to move toward loving kindness despite ridicule, criticism, hate, or persecution. Love should feel natural and kind. Approaching life with love and compassion opens the heart to new opportunities for growth. People hold emotions and fears within their hearts; perhaps those places of malice and fear that are unseen become seen only with the expression of anger. Approaching the inner child or the inner critic with a sense of understanding and acceptance can be the first step toward healing.

We can find ways to accept love by framing things in a new way or seeing things from a new perspective. Cognitive behavioral therapy invites opportunities to adopt new perspectives or a view from a new position, which can be a great mode of therapy for people working with trauma. Sometimes when people are emotionally or physically hurt, they find it hard to accept love. Creating a new view or entry point for letting love in and opening the heart may require vulnerability. It is hard to be vulnerable without feeling trust in the relationship with the loving recipient. According to *A General Theory of Love* (2000), love makes us who we are and who we can become; and while love emanates from our brain's cognitions, it is held in the heart (Lewis et al., 2007).

Buddhist meditation instructor Sharon Salzberg (2017) has said, "We are born ready to love and be loved. It is our birth right" (p. 11). However, as we live and grow, "suffering might be some kind of credential" (p. 32), the yin to the yang of love. Suffering exists so we may truly know the capacity of love after seeing such suffering. "To truly love ourselves we must be open to wholeness, rather than clinging to slivers of ourselves represented by old stories" (p. 32).

Before my father's symptoms began to really present themselves, about a couple of weeks before he died, he had a deep and loving glimmer in his eye –a look of genuine care and compassion. I saw the deepest love emanate from him when he looked at his two grandchildren, Ezra and Daisy. My sister and I were pregnant at the same time, and her daughter was born just 10 weeks before my son. With two babies in the family, my father was ever present, eager, and focused on being the world's greatest grandpa. His heart was locked on his grandchildren and radiating the most pure love for them.

Sometimes the beams of love in our life are not what we planned for. Phoebe and Jeff, two artists, wanted to grow their family.

But despite medical treatments and lots of trying, they were not able to conceive on their own (Potts, 2010). Phoebe and Jeff told me that adopting their son from Ethiopia ended a cycle of familial abuse through generations of inherited trauma. There was a separation in the trauma because the womb was different. The people who can see you as you are and love all of you no matter who you are—are what makes a family. The people who stick by you thick and thin are your family. Family does not have to be the people you are related to, a "home for the holidays" ideal exploited by Target holiday commercials. As Phoebe said to me, the people who celebrate you and take you in and ask for your support—this is family.

Phoebe and Jeff are fully aware that their son has birth parents, that a woman gave birth to him and had to decide whether to raise him. Though they did not make their son, he is their family. He is also from Ethiopia. For this reason, they feel a connection to that region and a responsibility to the people there.

They have been looking for his genetic relatives to help build their son's story. They realize that even if they do not find their son's relatives, some connection to his place of birth can be found through other adoptees. They have therefore connected with other families who have adopted children from that region. It can be powerful for a child to have a sense of the community they came from, and having that connection can help heal the wound of separation (P. Potts, & J. Marshall, personal communication, December 28, 2020). And by healing his wound, Phoebe and Jeff hope their son can fully receive their love.

It is love that sustains us and allows us to bloom. It is love that gives us a chance to share our stories, heal our hearts, and grow.

Our heart always exceeds us.

—Rilke, *Second Elegy*

Conceptualizing Home

Confronting the question of where we come from, our home, can provoke many internal questions. I ask my students to use art, music, and dance to create a personal representation on the theme of home. Sitting on the floor of her dorm room and thinking about what home meant to her, Danii arrived at "Home is where the heart is." She questioned what is in her heart and where her home is as she reflected on her parents' sudden and unexpected divorce in the summer before she attended college. The divorce, she recalled, split her entire family and deteriorated her relationship with her father.

The night before her debut in the college musical, she hoped that someone in her family would show up, but no one did. Instead, her five best friends from college came to all five performances that week with a bouquet each night. She said, "Friends are the family that you choose." Our family of origin is not necessarily the people we choose to be with—we are just automatically bound to them through our ancestral roots. In her reflection, Danii created a work of art that showed colored patterns representing the coordinates and location of her family of origin and her friends at college. The colors were drawn over a heart with bloodlines connecting to everyone on her heart map, which she decorated with petals her friends had given to her after her debut performance.

Israeli expressive arts therapist Dana Albert-Proos (2015) worked with immigrant expressive therapists to learn more about the perception of home and reconstructing home. For Albert-Proos, an immigrant herself, adjusting to a new culture and identifying the meaning of home was near and dear to her heart. Her arts-based research involved semistructured interviews, art making, and written reflection with 10 practicing expressive therapists. Based on the participants' responses, Albert-Proos identified metaphors and quotes and ultimately made a film. Qualitative analysis of the interviews, art, and reflections yielded three themes related to home: belonging and not belonging; home here and home there, home nowhere and home everywhere; and old me and new me (evolution of identity). She found that the art making, reflection, and conversation allowed for meaning-making to understand and reconstruct what home means to immigrant expressive therapists.

Home for humans, hopefully, can be a place where we feel safe, where we are cared for, and where we hold memories or roots. When people ask you where your home is, how do you respond? Perhaps home is where you grew up or where your family lives, but if your home has been destroyed, does that make home an ethereal place? Perhaps home can be a place within only when all walls and doors have been ruined. As Gibran wrote:

> You shall not dwell in tombs made by the dead for the living. And though of magnificence and splendor, your house shall not hold your secret nor shelter your longing. For that which is boundless in you abides in the mansion of the sky, whose door is the morning mist and whose windows are the songs and the silences of the night. (Gibran, 1923/1951, pp. 33–34)

Awakening Resilience

Austrian psychiatrist Viktor Frankl, who was imprisoned at Auschwitz, believed the key to existence is finding its purpose and deeper meaning. This philosophy helped Frankl comfort himself and his fellow prisoners after they were torn from their homes and their families under the Nazi regime. In his seminal book, *Man's Search for Meaning*, Frankl (2006/1962) recounts his experience of the Holocaust and what helped him survive. Such stories have inspired others to explore meaning and resiliency in the most horrific situations. In her memoir, *The Choice*, Edith Egar (2018), described her ability as a Holocaust survivor to transcend all of the guilt, shame, and anger she has felt. Eger's parents were ripped away from her and killed in a gas chamber in Auschwitz. Egar was discovered by the Nazis in 1945 under a pile of dead bodies. To survive, she used her talents as a professional ballet dancer, performing for Nazi officers just to stay alive. Later, Egar used her knowledge and experience and became a world-renowned clinician, helping others struggling with PTSD.

During the COVID-19 pandemic, when we all feared infection, I kept reminding my family and my students that we cannot control what others do, we can only control how we respond as individuals. The more resilient we are, the better and quicker we can recover from struggles. We all experience trauma. The key is learning how to live with the changes in our life due to it. During the pandemic, the phrase "living with the new normal" became common to describe mask wearing, vigilant sanitizing, and minimizing public exposure. We were able, with the support and modeling of all people, to adapt as best as we could to the flow of things. We tried our best to accept both those who resisted and those who continued to wear masks after the restrictions stopped doing so without judgment.

Israeli American expressive arts therapist Tamar Einstein said, "Right now, we are going through shared trauma, considering this COVID-19 pandemic as a shared trauma. Trauma means that you know that there was a before and after [trauma] (BT and AT). No one is ever going to be able to say that there was no coronavirus (BC and AC). We are all going through this collective trauma, besides the fact that this is scary and horrible, the arts are very anchoring at this period in time" (T. Einstein, personal communication, July 20, 2020).

Yousef AlAjarma a Palestinian expressive arts therapist and professor at William James College in Newton, Massachusetts, specializes in using the arts for resiliency and trauma. Yousef recalls his childhood growing up in Palestine as one fraught with instability, political contention, and exposure to extreme violence. He was born into a large family in the middle of 13 brothers and sisters, who all lived at a refugee camp near Bethlehem, Palestine. At the age of six, he began working at a vegetable market and gave all of his earnings to his father to provide food for his family. When he was a teenager, he began to fight in the resistance and was arrested and imprisoned in Israel for two years, just for throwing rocks at an Israeli building. He was able to cope with the imprisonment by making art, using whatever he had. He carved discarded olive pits and stones that he found on the ground, pieced together bits of plastic, and wrote poems.

Yousef said that building resilience during childhood can help prevent the pitfalls of trauma. As a young boy, he learned that he had to fight the occupation with education. He educated himself as a therapist and scholar. He has focused his life's work on the use of art to build resilience among individuals in conflict, especially Palestinians, through community, family, and education (AlAjarma, 2010).

Resiliency can begin with a strong community and good education. Writer Alison Gopnik (2021) wrote an op-ed in the *Wall Street Journal* reflecting on the value of a free preschool program that Boston public schools initiated in 1997. When the schools began to offer this free program, there was one problem. There were not enough placements for all preschool-age children, so the solution was to create a random lottery to determine which children could attend these schools. The majority of students who participated were Black or Latino, and many received free lunch services. Boston followed up on these students 20 years later to compare the success of the 4,000 students who had won the lottery with those who had not attended the public preschool. Those who went through Boston's public preschool lottery program as children were more likely to have graduated from high school, taken SAT tests, and gone to college than those who had attended Head Start programs, which did not show an impact on future or long-term success. They were also less likely than other groups to have been suspended or incarcerated. Many preschools teach academic skills; however, one of the major differences in the Boston preschools was the emphasis on play and creativity, combined with deeply caring teachers. Engaging the children early in creativity and play ultimately made them more robust and resilient and put them on the best path for success.

Psychologist and expert on emotional intelligence Daniel Goleman (2012) explains that the nervous system typically adapts to its environment but that people who have been exposed to trauma have different nervous systems. Our development maps out how we respond to stress and how resilient we are. Since early 2020, the human race has suffered ongoing collective trauma: the lockdowns, the lives lost due to the pandemic, riots, violence, political division, inconsistent policies and adherence (masks or no masks, vaccine or no vaccine), and a crashing economy. The brain can lag in its ability to adapt to all of the changes. And people's brains are foggy with the complexities of the more than two years of uncertainty. Now is the time for resilience and for connecting with and nourishing the child within; now is the time to yield to what is easy and to stand up when we need to. Optimism, spirit, emotional flexibility, and social belongingness can help keep us more resilient, but sometimes when those resources are not in reach, we need to dig deep into the heart of our internal creative resources. We have an awareness within us that leads our heart and soul to their destination. We just need to listen to where we are being led and maybe let music be our guide.

Companion Listening #9

"Hallelujah" by Leonard Cohen (1984; as sung by Jeff Buckley, 1994)

Creative Exercise #9: Sacred Rituals

Rituals are routines or traditions that you may practice time and time again to bring psychological and spiritual nurturance, community, and resilience. During the pandemic, there was a loss of rituals, loss of being together, and loss of touch. The word *ritual* lives within the word *spiritual*. However, rituals do not need a spiritual or sacred meaning; rituals can be practiced just to make you feel good. Some of the rituals we practice can become lost in the daily business of life, but practicing rituals can keep us grounded and connected to our ancestors, our health, and our belonging. This exercise allows you to consider those rituals that are most sacred to you.

Perhaps your ritual might be to take a cold shower in the morning or a drink a cup of tea before bed; maybe you have a ritual in which you prepare your meals or say goodnight to your family. Rituals can be inherited, given, or acquired. To begin this exercise, grab a pen and paper and begin to list your family, daily, and yearning rituals.

- Family rituals: Make a list of your longest-kept family rituals, those that have been practiced for some time, either in your current family or perhaps the rituals that ground you in your ancestry. These are the rituals that bring community and a sense of tradition. Include everything from the way you celebrate holidays to how you honor birthdays and death dates.

- Daily rituals: Make a list of the daily rituals that you practice for yourself. These are the rituals that you may practice on your own to bring personal nurturance and calm. Perhaps it is the ritual of going to bed at a certain time, the way you wash your hands, or prepare your breakfast.

- Yearning rituals: These are the rituals that cultivate health and resilience, to make you stronger for the future. Perhaps these are creative, healthful habits such as playing music each morning, taking a brisk walk on New Year's Day, or writing letters to friends.

Once you have listed all of your rituals, on a new piece of paper, draw a line or a mark that represents you. Around the "you" mark, draw marks that represent all of your family rituals. The marks can take any form or shape, and they can be placed closer or farther from the "you" mark depending on how you feel about the ritual. Do the same with your daily and yearning rituals. After creating all of the marks, notice how long or short, wavy or straight those marks are and how far or close they are from the "you" mark. Next, think about the shape and proximity of the marks to the "you" mark as a metaphor for your relationship with that ritual. Allow your marks to serve as a map or creative record to show you the rituals that are most important to you.

Here are some of my own sacred rituals: *lighting Shabbat candles, lighting yahrzeit candles, saying a goodnight prayer, drinking one cup of tea and one cup of coffee in the morning, writing a letter to the mothers I know on Mother's Day, lighting the Hanukkah candles, visiting with Tamar in the summertime, celebrating every birthday with cake and candles, saying "I love you," . . . keeping a journal, creating a photo album after every trip.*

References

AlAjarma, Y. (2010). *The role of the arts toward healing trauma and building resilience in the Palestinian community* [Doctoral dissertation, Lesley University]. *Expressive Therapies Dissertations* 34. https://digitalcommons.lesley.edu/expressive dissertations/34

Albert-Proos, D. (2015). *Separation from and reconstruction of home: A study of immigrant expressive therapists* [Doctoral dissertation, Lesley University]. *Expressive Therapies Dissertations* 68. https://digitalcommons.lesley.edu/expressive dissertations/68

American Polarity Therapy Association. (2021, June 30). *Origins of polarity therapy.* https://polaritytherapy.org/about/history/

Blake, W. (2021). *The songs of innocence and of experience.* Independently published. (Original work published 1789)

Carducci, B. J. (2009). *The psychology of personality: Viewpoints, research, and applications.* Brooks / Cole Publishing Company.

Demaine, K. (2018). The radiant fire: Confronting the critic and nurturing the inner child. In E. Scholz (Ed.), *Anxiety Warrior: Volume Two* (pp. 151–162). The Artist's Reply.

Egar, E. (2018). *The choice: Embrace the possible.* Schribner.

Farmer, S. (2014). *Healing ancestral karma: Free yourself from unhealthy family patterns.* Hierophant Publishing.

Frankl, V. (2006). *Man's search for meaning.* Beacon Press. (Original work published 1962)

Gibran, K. (1951). *The prophet.* Alfred A. Knopf. (Original work published 1923)

Goleman, D. (2012). *Emotional intelligence: Why it can matter more than IQ* (10th anniversary ed.). Bantam Dell.

Gopnik, A. (2021). Preschool's "sleeper" effect on later life. *Wall Street Journal.* https://www.wsj.com/articles/preschools-sleeper-effect-on-later-life-11622146543

Hanh, T. N. (2014). *No mud, no lotus.* Parallax Press.

Henson, J., & Oz, F. (Directors). (1982). *The dark crystal* [Film]. ITC Entertainment Henson Associates.

Hillman, J. (1996). *The soul's code.* Bantam.

Hoffman, R. (2020, May 17). *Alfred Adler's theories of individual psychology and Adlerian therapy.* Simply Psychology. https://www.simplypsychology.org/alfred-adler.html

Huron, D. (2007). *Sweet anticipation: Music and the psychology of expectation.* MIT Press.

Katie, B., & Mitchell, S. (2002). *Loving from within: Four questions that can change your life.* Harmony Books.

Lewis, T., Amini, F., & Lannon, R. (2007). *A general theory of love.* Vintage Publishers.

Potts, P. (2010). *Good eggs: A memoir.* Harper Collins.

Seuss, Dr. (1957). *How the Grinch stole Christmas.* Random House.

Solomon, A. (2012). *Far from the tree: Parents, children, and the search for identity.* Scribner.

Chapter 10

Living with a Conscious Heart

To truly love ourselves, we must treat our stories with respect,
but not allow them to have a stranglehold on us,
so that we free our mutable present and beckoning future from the past.
—Sharon Salzberg, *Real Love: The Art of Mindful Connection*

The Seat of the Soul

In the days after my father died, I spent nearly every daytime hour with my mom and sisters planning out his memorial service and trying to make sense of everything. We sat shiva, in our own way, as a family. My mom did not want visitors, but visitors stopped by her home anyway. In the Jewish tradition, after a person dies, a weeklong mourning period, called shiva allows immediate family members to sit quietly at home and accept visitors for discussion and contemplation as part of the grieving ritual. There is something conscious and deliberate about sitting shiva, with the opportunity to pause and reflect. One day during a drive home, after sitting and being with my mother, my son held out his little hand to me and said, "I made this when we came home from the hospital, when Guppa was dying. This is his brain-heart—it has his spiritual energy in it." He uncurled his tiny hand and inside was a swirling pile of red twist ties from which he had created the "brain-heart" (shown below). He had carried the small sculpture home, clutching it during the 30-minute car ride without saying a word.

My son and my niece—my sister's daughter—were both five years old when my father died. When my sister's daughter arrived at the hospital, my son said to her, "Guppa's broken and they can't fix him—he's dying." While my son was speaking a language that his cousin could understand, his message was so poignant. Just two days after Dad died, his physical body was transported away to be converted to ash. It was amazing to me how quickly the body is transformed from animation to stillness, perhaps to a place of return from where life once began, perhaps a different kind of energy, or to a spiritual place. As so many religions remind us, we are all ultimately dust.

Figure 9. *Guppa's Brain-Heart*, 2019. Paper-coated wire twist ties, 1.5 x 1.5 in. Artist: Ezra Demaine. Reproduced by permission from Ezra Demaine.

Ancient Egyptians believed that the heart was the seat of the soul and the key to the afterlife (Brandt & Huppert, 2021). The heart was said to be the first part of us that travels from the spirit world into the physical body—as it is the first functional organ to fully develop in the human fetus. Spiritual energy healer Alex Telman (2015) says that the soul exists in the human body in the form of a spirit. In essence, Telman believes that the soul and spirit are two separate entities that rely on one another during human life. In the afterlife, the spirit peels out of the soul; the soul does not cross over to a separate world with the spirit. While the spirit resides in the body during human life, the true home of the spirit is a spiritual world outside of the human body to which the spirit returns in the afterlife. Telman says that the spirit learns through experiences, especially those that are most painful. When the human body dies, some souls do not cross back over to the spirit world because of confusion or unresolved issues; some souls become stuck, at least for some time, before transitioning to the other side. Kirlian photography, a method of photographing gas discharge, developed by Russian physicist Konstantin Korotkov, is the first imaging method to supposedly capture the soul leaving the body. The soul can be seen rising above the body, gradually, first by the head and navel, followed by the groin, and last, the heart—the energetic center. Recalling the ancient Egyptian practice of leaving the heart intact during mummification, Kirlian photography has shown that it is the heart that stays with the body the longest during the transition from life to death.

Changing of the Guard

On January 6, 2019, my family held a memorial service for my father at our synagogue. Before the service began, my sisters and I waited in a small room with our children, our mother, and our father's siblings. I held my young son tight in my arms as he clung to my chest and wrapped his legs around my torso. One by one, the rabbi pinned a black piece of fabric over each of our hearts and then tore it in half. The tearing of the kriah symbolizes the expression of grief by the person who wears the torn fabric. Outside of the room, photos of Dad and our family together filled the atrium of the synagogue. Memories of his youth, his music, his loves, and his life. On a table, there were more photographs in frames and a glass container with 100 stone hearts, and a sign I had created that read *"Please accept an amazonite healing heart . . . The colors represent the birthstone of Ken Demaine. Amazonite is charged to offer healing, clarity, creativity, truth, and purpose."*

We expected 75 people to attend Dad's memorial service, and more than 300 showed up. Word travels fast for a beloved man in a small community. The blur of the afternoon, a large party hosted in solemnity, was like a dream. The rabbi sang Hebrew prayers; my sisters shared stories and stood next to me while I sang an arrangement of Beatles songs at the podium. My son sat in the front row staring at me, his eyes glazed, and sitting next to my mother, who was like a weeping stone. When the services concluded, we were greeted one by one by visitors standing in long lines; there were fond conversations with my father's former bandmates, employees of my parents' gift shop, and kids (who were now adults) that were musically inspired by my father.

In the weeks and months after my dad died, I continued to go to my parents' house and play his guitars. They were like old friends, and I felt like his guitars needed a visit just as my mom did. His Martin D18 dreadnought, always a bit too big for my hands, spoke to me. When I picked up the guitar, the Beatles' "Norwegian Wood" and "You've Got to Hide Your Love Away" poured out of my fingers, and I sang the melodies, my head leaning over and my ear pressed on the side of the guitar—as if hugging my father. I began to anthropomorphize his other musical instruments as if they were him. My sisters continued to feel his living energy in my parents' apartment. In those early days, Mom refused to leave the apartment because she felt so strongly that by leaving the space, she would be abandoning Dad.

I always kept a flute in my dad's music room just in case we wanted to play some jazz standards together. About six months before my dad died, he returned my flute to me. Around that same time, my dad stopped performing music with the bands he was playing in. He slowly withdrew from playing with people and at home. I have a photo of my dad showing my son how to play the autoharp a few months before he died. I have memories of Dad playing his upright bass a bit before that time and singing and playing ukulele with the grandkids a bit before then. The shift in my dad's engagement with playing music was palpable. There was a changing of the guard—Dad had become relieved of his duties.

A full year after my father died, almost to the day, our dog of almost 16 years also died. When Sage left us, my son and I had several existential conversations. He said, "I wonder if we enter into another portal or experience when we die, maybe there is a place that our spirit transitions to, through a unique entry, like on a rainbow or a beam of light."

In peace, Sage
(May 24, 2004–December 22, 2019)

The River of Consciousness

All things that go in and out of this world, in life and death, may fall through a river of consciousness. The question of whether consciousness exists after death has been widely contemplated, by everyone including scientists, theorists, and spiritualists. Science presumes that consciousness ends when the physical brain stops working. It understands that consciousness is matter and that when energetic matter dies, there is simply no more existence. Therefore, when the brain stops functioning, we can no longer possess consciousness, according to this view. Yet in other views, consciousness is said to continue after death.

When we sleep, we are unconscious of most things around us, but we can be woken into a conscious state of awareness. It is not unlike if we have fainted or if we are in a coma, from which we are not as easily aroused. As discussed in chapter 4, sleep is deeply important to human health, impacting nearly all human organs, the immune system, and emotional function. Neuroscientist Antonio Damasio (2011) suggests that every morning when we wake up, we regain a sense of consciousness, a new conscious mind. Consciousness is dependent on the brain stem, the stalk-like part of the brain that connects the brain with the spinal cord and houses all of the body's vital life functions, like breathing, heartbeat, and blood pressure. When part of this region is damaged by a stroke or another brain trauma, possibly even resulting in a coma, consciousness can disappear. The interconnectivity between the brain stem, the brain, and the body is what makes possible the conscious mind and self-awareness. Every day is a new day, and a chance to reset and restart with a new conscious frame of mind.

The notion that consciousness is stored solely in the brain has been challenged by researchers. This is in part because electrical signals and neurons exist in organs other than the brain, including the heart, liver, and lungs. The existence of this neuroelectrical activity suggests that consciousness can exist in these other organs of the body. Consciousness involves sensations, thoughts, feelings, and awareness of existence. This backs the idea of why we feel emotions in our heart and why we may follow our heart to make conscious decisions. This also supports recent research in and advancement of social-emotional awareness and efforts in diverse fields to encourage greater mind-heart connection.

A central question for many researchers is *where does consciousness go when we die?* Clinically, we understand that death occurs when the heart stops beating. We hear about near-death experiences in which a person is brought back to life after their heart stops by CPR or other medical interventions. We understand that the heart can at times be restarted, but what about restarting consciousness? Scientists have shown that neurons are resilient and that their lifespan extends past the functionality of the heart. In other words, after the heart stops beating and the body is presumed dead, neural consciousness continues. In 2017, a group of researchers discovered among mice and zebrafish that neural activity not only continued after heart death but the activity spiked after the heart died (Pozhitkov et al., 2016). The increased neural activity may explain the white light that people reportedly see in near-death experiences, but there has not been a way to measure this. Similar neural activity has been recorded in humans with no pulse detected and no heartbeat. Even when all functioning ceased to exist, neuroimaging continued to detect electrical activity.

When the heart stops beating, oxygen is no longer distributed throughout the cells in the body, including in the brain, which in turn causes brain damage. However, if brain cells are alive and active, partial brain functionality can remain. In April 2019, a group of researchers at Yale University reported that they had been able to keep pigs' brains alive outside of their bodies for six hours, which prompted the question of the reversibility of death (Vrselja et al., 2019). During the six hours, the Yale researchers reported that the pigs' brains were able to maintain immune and metabolic functions while receiving a nutrient and oxygen-based solution. The brains that did not receive the solution failed to survive. Electrical activity did not continue in either the treated or control brains past the six hours, but researchers claimed it could have if the brains had received an electric shock, kind of like jump-starting a car.

The field of quantum physics supposes that there is no separation between energy and matter, that when we die, energy does not go away, it just changes. We may consider the energy as being disorganized but not gone. I wonder if there is a river of consciousness, a place where all sensations of awareness go? Mediums create a meeting space for both worlds to be united. When my father died, I met with a medium who seemed to connect my father to me relatively quickly. She was able to tell me things that only my father had experienced in his last days of living, things that I thought only he was aware of came back to me through this medium. If consciousness is ethereal, it is the medium that communicates with the energetic consciousness after it leaves the body. When someone dies, I believe that person's energy goes back into the universe and into the river of consciousness that vibrates with the lives of our ancestors.

Stories of afterlife experiences by people who have been on the brink of death share certain details, that they left their body and transitioned to another realm. Raymond Moody's book *Life after Life* (1975) told some of the first modern-day stories of near-death experiences. All of the experiences reported were anecdotal in nature and lack scientific reliability. However, Moody identified common themes from the people who had near-death experiences, a term he coined, which in turn suggested predictability and therefore more scientific reliability. Some people who have been deemed clinically dead can see and hear things in the room that are not possible to be seen. Moody's book chronicled the first experiences of seeing the white light, which, as mentioned earlier has been reported by many more people since and has often been portrayed in films.

Psychologist Brian Weiss treats patients working through traumas caused by past-life experiences. In his classic book *Many Lives, Many Masters* (1988), Weiss shares the story of an early patient who opened his eyes to the possibility that a person's current stress could originate from a past-life experience. The patient, Katherine, came into Weiss's office suffering from fears and phobia, specifically fear of choking, which prevented her from taking her medicine. Weiss tried traditional psychotherapy with Katherine, and after making little progress, Weiss tried hypnosis, a method he later developed as past-life regression therapy. The hypnosis put Katherine in a state of relaxed concentration. In this subconscious state, people can recall memories that often are not accessed during wakeful consciousness. Weiss instructed Katherine, in the subconscious state, to go to the time when she first choked. In doing so, Katherine remembered a past life from the Middle Ages, a life that was not hers and that she was not biologically related to. When she confronted the story, she was able to deal with the issue and separate the feelings associated with this person from a past life. It is almost as if the energy had become entangled in the conscious and unconscious worlds. Weiss's method in past-life therapy has helped hundreds of people. Past-life regression therapy is different from working with ancestral trauma, which comes from biological lineage. By contrast, in past-life therapy, the person experiencing the trauma does not necessarily have any heritable relationship with the person that is connected to the pain.

In a 2005 interview on NPR's *All Things Considered*, physicist Aaron Freeman explained the notion that energy does not die: "You want a physicist to speak at your funeral. You want the physicist to talk to your grieving family about the conservation of energy, so they will understand that your energy has not died" (Norris, 2015, 00:10). The notion that energy exists as vibration is a compelling concept. However, when someone dies, we keep that thread of connection in many ways, through energy, through memory, and sometimes through matter, holding those physical treasures close to us for as long as we can, continuing the life of the person who has died.

Messages of Affirmation

When someone dies, there may be messages that we receive from them, hopefully giving us a chance to find some solace or continued connection. These signals may serve as a reminder that we are all connected by the energy of the universe. When my father died, I started to receive what I thought were electric musical signals from him. The signs that I received came through objects powered by electricity. Energy and vibration run through all things, creating a connection between ourselves and electrical devices. I began to notice an unveiling or an unfolding of things, and I felt a true and near connection to my father.

In her book *What the Dead Have Taught Me about Living Well*, author Rebecca Rosen (2017) says:

> It is easy for spirits to manipulate electricity and cross wires, so to speak, because both spirits and electricity are forms of energy that vibrate at a high frequency and are highly charged. Look for lights flickering in the house, lightbulbs blowing out, or disturbance with television sets, radios, appliances and computers. These are all typical spirit moves, and often just their way of saying hello. (p. 188)

Rosen notes that children and toddlers are also able to communicate with the spirit world. When children talk about the spirit world, it is important to listen without judgment and encourage them to speak what they believe to be true. It is important to bring children to nature to connect better with the spiritual world. Biking, swimming, and walking through natural outdoor environments can bring a greater connection to universal consciousness.

One night after visiting family and just a short time after Dad died, my sister sent a text message on our family chat with a photo of her Quick Pick lottery ticket. Of the five numbers that were automatically selected by the computer, the first three were my father's birthday month, day, and year: 6-16-53. Feeling like this was a sign from Dad, my son and I stopped a few moments later at the nearest convenience store on our ride home. We bought a Quick Pick ticket, just as my sister had, and could not believe the numbers that the machine sputtered out. The ticket read 8-16-17-50-53. Each number had significant meaning to me. The first number, 8, is my mother's birth day, 16 is my father's and son's birth day, 17 is my birth day, 50 is the number of years my parents had been together, and 53 is my father's birth year. I thought for sure that these numbers were a sign from my dad.

After that day, more electrically driven and synchronous experiences began to occur. The radio in my new car began to spontaneously turn on and off as I was driving home from visiting my mom. When the radio did finally turn on, it played classic rock and always something that my father would have listened to, a song from *Disraeli Gears* by Cream or by the Beatles. The same thing began to occur at my house with Alexa devices; without any prompt, Alexa would begin to play kirtan music (yoga chant music). Around that time, I started to create a musical life review for my dad, chronologizing the songs that had played a role in his life. Those songs started to spontaneously play on my Alexa device as well.

In their book *Hello from Heaven*, Bill Guggenheim and Judy Guggenheim (1997) interviewed people who had experienced the death of a family member and collected 3,300 accounts of spontaneous after death communication (ADC). The family members believed they had seen, heard, or felt the presence of a person who had died. Psychology has pointed to these ADCs as grief hallucinations. The ADC experiences that grieving individuals experience exemplify the power of the imagination or the brain's attempt to make sense of the loss, but they also may provide comfort for the grieving person who may sense that their loved one is safe. Many clinical observers of death, theologians, and spiritualists believe that death is simply a transition from life to a different realm. When we are exposed to death, we begin to notice new things that we did not previously tune into—there may be a new sense of intuitive awareness. As my son said, "The spirit dragon guides on with you." There is something powerful and bold that can accompany the grief journey if we so allow it.

On March 21, 2019, during a car ride home from his school, my son said to me, "Mommy, there are spiritual signs all around you." He then told me, "The heart contains spirit energy." The following night, after Shabbat dinner, my son and I sat on the couch together; the house was quiet, and with Dad's yahrzeit candle lit, we began talking about him. I found my son's words so riveting that I grabbed a notepad, as I often do, and started writing down what he was saying. My son said about my dad, "*He goes where we go, he protects us . . . His spirit guides us on. The spirit man guides on with us.*" He paused and then said, "*Guppa sent me a message just now. He said that he'll do stuff to let Bubbie [my mom] know that he is still there.*" He paused again while I sat in silence, and then as if talking to somebody else, my son said, "*So, it's all fine.*" My son paused, then said, "*Guppa is mad about us talking about him!*" After sitting quietly and only listening and writing down what he was saying, I finally asked my son, "*Why is Guppa mad?*" My son said, "*Guppa is pulling out one screen of my memories.*" I asked what my son meant and where the screen came from. My son pointed to the top of his head and quickly he held up his hand and said, "*Stop, Mommy . . . Just stop, Mommy.*" Then at that very moment, my cell phone lit up with a text message from my *dad's* phone number! The text message simply said, "*I'm fine.*"

I tried to rationalize scientifically this message I received from my dad. It was two and a half months after my father had died and two full months since his cell phone had been disabled and his phone

143

number canceled. The phenomenon chilled me and soothed me all at once. My dad is fine. I told a dear friend some of these experiences I was having and she responded, "You have been very deeply connected to parts of your consciousness and the universe's consciousness that are not usually apparent or accessible. Such openness allows for open communication. It is calming to know he is now fine. And maybe your son can feel that now you can continue to live, love, thrive, and grow with your father as a protector who is at rest now . . . Life is full of potential we never tap into. You are experiencing rare synchronicities. Cherish them" (T. Einstein, personal communication, January 12, 2019).

The Sacred Chant

Music therapist Kenneth Aigen (2019) wrote in memory of his wife, Benedikte Scheiby, "Having been raised by an alcoholic mother and suicide killed father, her life was impoverished." Aigen was amazed how his wife, given the circumstances, developed into a pioneering music therapist, a mother, and a surrogate mother for so many of her beloved students. "She refused to be a victim of her history," said Aigen (p. 5). Shieby left a legacy of music and healing for which she touched many lives in a most sacred and meaningful way.

A few weeks after my dad died, one of his friends sent my mother a recording of him singing "Green Eyes" by Coldplay. My mom, who had never heard the song, assumed that my dad's friend had written the song for her. She imagined my dad singing to her about her green eyes. The image conjured a sense of connection to my dad, something that was difficult for her to feel after he had died. This container of music was a comfort and reassurance to my mom.

Music seems to find its way to the connections binding people together, through the universe and beyond. It can give us a place to let our hearts sing and feel held and comforted. When we experience grief, we sometimes look for these connections or communications, but as psychologist Francis Weller (2015) points out, when someone dies, a veil is lifted and we begin to see things with a new perspective; things simply seem to reveal themselves to us with pure clarity. In grief, we are somehow open to receiving new messages and experiences, and it becomes clear that the energy of the person is still all around even after death. Grief has no timeline, and you cannot pretend that it is not there. Sometimes when things are at their hardest, we can see most clearly.

On a whim and with lots of luck, just a month and a half after Dad died, on February 16, 2019, I had the opportunity to see my favorite kirtan singer, Snatam Kaur, perform in concert. Snatam Kaur's music had been important to me when I was in labor and delivery with my baby and was something that carried me when my father died. What I could not believe was that Snatam was performing in my small hometown of Rockport, Massachusetts. When I found out about her performance, I quickly called the performance center to book tickets, which I found out were sold out. I tracked down the phone number for Kaur's booking manager and shared my story about Dad, my son, and the importance of this sacred music in my life. The booking manager was able to pull some strings and secure seats for me and my sister and permission for my son to sit on my lap. This was the first concert that Kaur's group performed after they played live at the Grammy Awards in 2019, when they were nominated for best New Age album. I thought it was magic that they chose to play in this 300-seat theater in a small seaside town with a view of the sea as their backdrop.

As my sister, son, and I entered the performance hall, Kaur's booking manager greeted us with warmth, almost like a dream, and as if she had known me for some time—it felt like a homecoming. Most special to me was that Kaur opened the concert with her song "Ong Namo," a chant written by Yogi Bajan. This was *the song* that so deeply carried me through my grief and, profoundly, the same chant song that spontaneously popped on and off my Alexa device after Dad died. I was so taken away by spirit when Snatam began to sing the lyrics of this sacred chant. The lyrics say, "A city on the water, beyond time and space" and recount a mother taking the reins, a coming home, and freeing each other with heart. Kaur's lyrics, to me, mean that my father is coming home . . . maybe to my mom or maybe to something in a spiritual place. The space where I am living now, in the absence of my father, is a place of spirit, creativity, emotion, and feeling. It is a dynamic space, both quiet and loud, soft and rough. It is a place where the veil has left and there is more fluidity between this, the living physical body plane, and the spiritual plane. There is more access here to phenomena and more acceptance of the unknown. There is more creativity and, in turn, more music. There is powerful synchrony that music provides to the senses and emotions, giving us a chance to feel loved and connected, without us even knowing it.

In my conscious awakening, I look at my son with his warm eyes and pureness of heart—a child I am raising entirely on my own—and I am filled with love and pride for him and his wisdom. His eyes remind me how important and precious life is and that it is my responsibility to raise him with kindness, consciousness, and love. I realize this love is to be cherished in this one life. I choose my son and he chose me. It is time to forgive, to move forward, to live. This is our way, this is our grace, in gratitude.

Companion Listening #10

"Space Oddity" by David Bowie (1969)

Creative Exercise #10: Letter to the Self and Other

Letter writing has become a lost art in the digital age. Instead of sending letters, we text, email, or post on an online platform to convey our message. This exercise allows us to engage in the lost art of letter writing. You will need paper and two envelopes. Choose paper that you like. I learned years ago that I enjoy paper with a connection to nature. I photocopy leaves and flowers onto plain paper or find a piece of white birch bark (Mother Nature's paper), which helps me feel grounded and closer to the origins of my spirit.

The first letter you write will be to yourself. Address the letter to yourself: "Dear _____." Include a date on the letter and write your address. Let yourself know where you are, what you are thinking, feeling, manifesting, how your heart is feeling, and what is happening in your life. When you are done with the letter, sign it, and seal it in an envelope. Tuck this letter in a special location, which will allow you to rediscover it some months or years from now.

The second letter will be written to another person. Think of someone you would like to say something to. A letter can be written to another person as a method of releasing its content back into the energy of the universe. Write the date and the address of the person at the top of the letter. Write your message clearly and articulately. Pour out all that you need to communicate, without holding back. When you are done with this letter, put it in the envelope and seal it up. Take the letter to a safe place where you can burn it in fire, perhaps a fireplace or a burning bowl. You may discard the ashes of the letter to the other in any place that suits you. I like to scatter the ashes of my letter into the sea. When you are burning the letter you say, "I release the contents of this letter." You can add what you are physically releasing, specific emotions, thoughts, feelings, manifestations, or memories . . .

References

Aigen, K. (2019). You are the music: The music therapy spirit of Benedikte Scheiby. *Voices: A World Forum for Music Therapy*, *19*(2), 1–5.

Brandt, T., & Huppert, D. (2021). Brain beats heart: A cross-cultural reflection. *Brain*, *144*(6), 1617–1620.

Damasio, A. (2011). *The quest to understand consciousness* [Video]. TED Conferences. https://www.ted.com/talks/antonio_damasio_the_quest_to _understand_consciousness#t-782584

Guggenheim, B., & Guggenheim, J. (1997). *Hello from heaven: A new field of research-after-death communication confirms that life and love are eternal.* Bantam Books.

Moody, R. (1975). *Life after life: The investigation of a phenomenon-survival of bodily death.* Mockingbird Books.

Norris, M. (Host). (2015, June 1). *Planning ahead can make a difference in the end* [Radio broadcast]. NPR. https://www.npr.org/templates/story/story.php?storyId=46 75953

Pozhitkov, A., Neme, R., Domzet-Loso, T., Leroux, B., Soni, S., Tautz, D., & Noble, P. (2016). Thanatotranscriptome: Genes actively expressed after organismal death. *Open Biology*, *7*(1). https://doi.org/10.1098/rsob.160267

Rosen, R. (2017). *What the dead have taught me about living well.* Rodale Books.

Salzberg, S. (2017). *Real love: The art of mindful connection.* Flatiron Books.

Telman, A. (2015). *The healer: Conversations with Alex Telman.* Xlibris Publishing.

Vrselja, Z., Daniele, S. G., Silbereis, J., Talpo, R. Morozov, Y. M., Sousa, A. M. M., Tanaka, B. S., Skarica, M., Pletikos, M., Kaur, N., Zhuang, Z. W., Liu, Z., Alkawadri, R., Sinusas, A. J., Latham, S. R., Waxman, S. G., & Sestan, N. Restoration of brain circulation and cellular functions hours post-mortem. *Nature*, *568*, 336–343. https://doi.org/10.1038/s41586-019-1099-1

Weiss, B. (1988). *Many lives, many masters.* Fireside.

Weller, F. (2015). *The wild edge of sorrow: Rituals of renewal and the sacred work of grief.* North Atlantic Books.

Chapter 11

The Radiant Heart

You're more open than you've ever been.
Take gentle, loving care of yourself.
Be tender with your heart.
—Melody Beattie, *Journey to the Heart*

The Heart's Awakening

Practicing mindful presence can lead to authenticity of self, intuition, inner knowing, and awakening of the heart. Intuitive healer Carolyn Myss says in her book *Anatomy of the Spirit* (1996) that we have an intuition or feeling in the heart that leads us to our purpose in life. Following the heart is the primary way to be authentic. Awakening authenticity can happen through presence. Mindful presence can occur in most everyday activities—in those quiet moments of life, like washing the dishes, doing the laundry, or preparing dinner. This presence brings us close to the heart. Through this heart awakening, we may discover that presence allows us to really see someone, to see the truth. When I look at my son, I see true love

You'll miss the best things if you keep your eyes shut.
—Dr. Seuss

Jon Kabat-Zinn, founder of the Center of Mindfulness in Medicine, Health Care, and Society at the University of Massachusetts Memorial Health, said, "Practice sharing the fullness of your being, your best self, your enthusiasm, your vitality, your spirit, your trust, your openness; above all, your presence. Share it with yourself, your family, with the world" (1994, p. 62). Part of finding your authentic voice—the true heart is in listening to yourself—drawing upon your heart's intuitive nature fuels a compassioned core. Being honest and true to your nature can lead to a more fulfilling life. Yoga instructor Baron Baptiste followed in his parents' footsteps by practicing and teaching yoga. Yoga awakened him to an inner sense of power—an internal fire. This internal fire was ignited by something Baptiste called his true north (Baptiste, 2016). As Abraham Maslow in his theory of the hierarchy of needs and James Hillman in *The Soul's Code* suggest (see chapter 9), by actualizing the true calling of our authentic self, we can create internal freedom that allows us to follow the heart and unfold into a deep awaking.

When life shows up for us, we find ways to embrace it. We can receive signs that we are doing something right or if there is something to avoid. It is just a matter of our being willing to listen to our intuition. Drawing upon our healthy protective heart sense, we can make good and mindful decisions. The greater presence of mind we have, the better equipped we are for living. Looking after our heart and nurturing it through creative and grounding experiences are key to staying resilient, strong, and protected. Remember that everything in the natural world, the sun, plants, mountains, and the human body, are all teeming with electromagnetic energy, and on an atomic level, everything is connected. We need to take care of our health and the vibrations that surround us. Drumming, singing, vocalizing, and movement keeps us connected to the good vibrations and to nurturing the awareness of the heart. If we tune into the vibrations of places, we can be our own conscious readers, if we just trust ourselves—our intuition.

Forgiveness

Sharon Salzberg (2017) says that the unresolved stories in our life become traumatic residues. The residues that get stuck to the windows of our life make things difficult to see, difficult to look past. The ability to move through pain, grief, and unfulfilled expectations can be a daunting task. However, the concept of moving through rather than dismissing or ignoring grief is key to healthy living. Forgiveness begins with the self and listening to the inner critic as well as finding the roots of our rhythm and nurturing the inner child. But how can we have compassion and empathy if we have been badly hurt?

In *A Well of Being: An Extraordinary Children's Book for Adults,* Jean-Pierre Weill (2016) reflects on the limits of our narratives and reminds us to live fully and find life in our everyday moments. The self-judgmental narratives that we develop when we internalize the criticism of others or when we reflect on harmful ancestral roots can inhibit us from living fully. We can still live with these narratives and continue to have self-compassion; however, it is important to recognize that our narratives are still being written. These chapters in our lives are only part of the story that we are creating moment by moment.

Tara Brach (2016) says that so many people are trapped in the cycle of nonforgiveness. The day that my dad slipped into a coma, the doctors said he was just sleeping. I thought something more involved was going on, and I asked the doctor if Dad was failing to thrive. The doctor denied my suggestion, and I did not further push my hunch. Dad was slipping away. It takes forgiveness of heart and self to be able to sit with unwanted emotions. If we can identify and give a name to our emotions, we are better equipped to know how to address them. Brené Brown (2015) says that to empathize with someone's experience, you must accept what the other believes to be true so that we can see ourselves in the other person's position. We have to draw on our vulnerability and courage to assert our positions and also need to draw upon vulnerable moments to hear another person's story. Without hearing a person express their truth or their story, we will not be able to know the authenticity of another's concern or feeling. Sharing our stories and having a chance to be heard without judgment, whether we are a child or an adult, can be a powerful and transformative experience toward understanding and forgiveness.

"Forgiving and being reconciled to our enemies or our loved ones are not about pretending that things are other than they are. It is not about patting one another on the back and turning a blind eye to the wrong. True reconciliation exposes the awfulness, the abuse, the hurt, the truth."

–Desmond Tutu

The Sacred Space Within

A mudra is a gesture made with the hands that can offer an energetic symbol of intention to sacred areas within the body. In Hinduism and Buddhism, there are almost 400 mudras. In the West, hand gestures can have various meanings. For example, in the United States, a thumbs-up is a sign of approval or appreciation, but in some cultures such as Iran and Afghanistan, a thumbs-up is seen as offensive, like giving the middle finger. Yet these hand gestures are not mudras as they are known in yogic culture. In Indian yogic culture, there is a sacred mudra called *anjali* mudra, known as the heart-centered mudra; this involves bringing the hands into a prayer position at the center of the heart. We see this prayer position in many cultures. In yoga, this mudra sets an intention for focus, calm, and equanimity to the body; it allows for tuning into the heart, which leads to listening to the breath. As the breath nourishes all organs of the body, taking a moment in *anjali* mudra allows all of the cells in the body a chance to recalibrate and vibrate in harmony.

Take a moment to listen to the heart with your hands in *anjali* mudra, or prayer pose. Notice how this may feel different than simply folding your hands over the heart space. Imagine as you listen to the heart with thumbs pressed on the sternum that there is an energy running up and down the spine. Draw your shoulders back and bow your head a little. Breathe in and breathe out. Allow yourself to welcome the flow of energy that this alignment brings to the body. Tune into your body, and listen for anything in your alignment that is blocked. When energy gets stuck or blocked in our body, we need to understand what the body is trying to communicate to us. Perhaps there is a pain or an emotional sensation that is not allowing us to be fully free in our bodies. Our bodies are vibrational energetic musical systems, and when that system is not in sync, we can begin to feel dissonance or pain. With proper alignment and energetic flow, our bodies can radiate openly like a beautiful symphony of sound in pure musical delight. Finding your inner mudra, the mudra that serves as your symbol is a way to express your authentic voice. Sometimes we can be awakened by an inner sense of internal empowerment, not something that is empowering over others but rather expressing an authentic self, your true north (Baptiste, 2016).

A great way to start feeling the vibrational energy of the body is through mudras. Another easy mudra to feel simple energy is *gyan* mudra, which is performed by touching the tip of the thumb with the index finger, palms facing up while holding the other fingers out gently. In this mudra, you can begin to tune into the electric vibration between the fingers. As you pull your fingers apart, centimeter by centimeter, begin to notice how the fingers are attracted to each other; in this posture, you can begin to notice the magnetism between your fingers.

Thich Nhat Hanh says we need to ask ourselves what is our deepest desire and what is our intention. Many of us go through life without conscious awareness, transient passengers through the day-to-day motions, without recognizing the deeper meaning. We need to have a chance to feel struggle now so that we can have blissful experiences in the future. We need to recognize the pains to allow us to move through them. The process of being present and living in the here and now allows for freedom and peace within our bodies, hearts, and souls.

Deep Listening

There is a saying in music therapy that the eye is the distractor. This statement underscores the relative nature of our senses and how much information we can receive in the electric impulses and sensory experiences through sound. Sometimes, we can receive more information by just listening rather than both listening and looking together. Sound produces physical vibrations that can be felt, heard, and sometimes seen.

One semester while I was teaching an introductory music therapy course, there was a blind student enrolled in the class. When we played in the drum circle, this particular student always knew when it was her turn to play, she had the ability to listen deeply, perhaps because her senses were more developed without vision. She seemed to recognize the pocket and the groove better than anyone else in the group. She may simply have had greater innate musical ability might than the other students, but her highly developed senses of hearing and touch were key. She also engaged with an emotional expression that was uninhibited and appeared deeply authentic. In this way, she differed from the other students who, visually registering their classmates' drumming, seemed to have more inhibition, perhaps self-judgment, while playing. When I asked each student how they felt playing in the drum circle, this student said that she could feel the music and the emotion in her heart and that she could feel it easily. I asked the class to close their own eyes while they were playing the drums, to first feel the vibrations with their hands, then allow the vibrations to move up the body, and finally to feel the music with their heart. When they closed their eyes, the other students were able to synchronize better with the group and to play more freely. With their nonvisual senses deeply engaged, the group of students truly let their hearts follow the beat; they let their hearts sing that day.

Full of Light

In yoga, a goal of meditation is to radiate everything and to become full of light, to find the most freeing vibrational frequency of the heart because, after all, we are all energy, we are all light. Can you imagine your heart full of light and emanating peace and warmth from your whole body? Yogi Bhajan (1929–2004) is known to have said, "When you understand who you are and what you are, your inner radiance projects into the universal radiance, and everything around you becomes creative and full of opportunity." Strengthening radiance begins from focusing within—not in an egocentric way of focusing inward but as a form of deep listening.

Deep listening acknowledges the self, awareness of self, and identity of self. Focusing promotes kindness of self. Freud (1930/2010) posited that internal gratification, also known as self-esteem, in excess could lead to narcissism. The delicate ego can survive up to a certain threshold of judgment; beyond that threshold, depression or mania can occur. A protective heart reminds the self to maintain a baseline sense of awareness and not be thrown into ego neglect or overindulgence. For artists, a reliance on external validation can form at an early age and can be tended to by the self-critic.

Figure 10. *Untitled*, 2019. Block print, acrylic and pastel on paper, 5 x 7 in. Artist: Sara Roizen. Reproduced by permission from Sara Roizen.

Compassion in the literal sense means to suffer together—the root of compassion is thus empathy. Compassion brings us together and allows us to carry our burdens, bringing more lightness of heart. When the heart feels empathy, an invisible string draws it to other hearts and tugs at our desire to be held. In Chinese culture, the heart is viewed as the master of the body. In Buddhist philosophy, the heart radiates spiritual thought. Return yourself to the heart—bring yourself back to the truth. To my son, energy looks like a spirit—he describes energy as white sparkling fractals of rainbowed light. My son believes this is a universal energy that can be felt and seen. When we sit in silence, we can feel the vibrational energy within us and around us—the energy that links the deepest core of ourselves, our roots, and our surroundings.

In Rainer Maria Rilke's famous *Letters to a Young Poet*, he responds with the simplest message to a curious young writer seeking advice: *follow your heart*. Whittled down to its essence, Rilke's message is an encouragement of mindful awareness, of looking toward the self for answers—and listening deeply. What does your heart bid you do? Rilke writes, "Dig into yourself for a deep answer. And if this answer rings out in assent if you meet this solemn question with a strong simple, 'I must,' then build your life in accordance with this necessity; your whole life, even into its humblest and most indifferent hour, must become a sign and witness to this impulse" (Rilke, 1929/2012, p. 5).

Your destiny is to follow the roots and rhythm of your heart, to do what you need to do, and be who you need to be. Listening to and connecting to the music of your heart will help you connect to the truer and deeper part of yourself. Cherish the life that you live, the story that you tell, and allow yourself to be heard and listened to by others. Those who are appreciative of others will be appreciated. Recognize that each person is unique and at times struggling to live authentically, vulnerably, and pure of heart. Acknowledge the mystery of your ancestors—find your rhythm, and your frequency, listen to your heart and protect it. Allow yourself to be free and full of light. Listen to music, play music, and be connected to the rhythm of all living things. Allow your positive vibrations to ripple into society for healing, bringing loving compassion to all those who may need it. This is how I will follow my rhythm and call upon my roots. This is how I share my story, chapter by chapter, and I encourage you to write yours.

> *Your future hasn't been written yet, no one's has.*
> *Your future is whatever you make it, so make it a good one.*
> —Back to the Future III (Zemeckis, 1990, 1:52:17)

Companion Listening #11

"I Will" by the Beatles (1968)

Creative Exercise #11: Gratitude Gift Giving

For the final creative exercise, you will share a gift with a person or people who have nurtured the roots to your rhythm. These gifts can be given to a living or nonliving person. Sometimes I leave gifts for my father at his altar. Let the gift be simple, intentional, and natural. Perhaps you may draw toward nature for your gift, maybe a bouquet of wild flowers, a handwritten letter, a poem, or maybe pass this book along to them. Remember that you have also nurtured yourself, so please remember to give yourself a gift as well. Gratitude for the self can be as simple as breathing in through your nose and saying a silent thank you to yourself, breathing out through the mouth saying a silent thank you to someone else, then noticing how you feel. Let the other person and yourself know that you are grateful for the compassion and nurturance in helping you cultivate your rhythm. Showing appreciation for yourself and for others helps build the heart. In gratitude . . .

Companion Listening #12

"Ramble On" by Led Zeppelin (1969)

References

Baptiste, B. (2016). *Perfectly imperfect: The art and soul of yoga practice.* Hay House.

Brach, T. (2016). *True refuge: Finding peace and freedom in your own awakened heart.* Penguin Random House.

Brown, B. (2015). *Daring greatly: How the courage to be vulnerable transforms the way we live, love, parent, and lead.* Avery.

Freud, S. (2010). *Civilization and its discontents.* W. W. Norton and Company. (Original work published 1930)

Hanh, T. N. (2006). *Present moment wonderful moment.* Parallax Press.

Hay, L. (1999). *Power thought cards: A 64-card deck.* Hay House.

Kabat-Zinn, J. (1994). *Wherever you go, there you are: Mindfulness meditation in everyday life.* Hachette Books.

Myss, C. (1997). *Anatomy of the spirit.* Harmony Books.

Rilke, R. M. (2012). *Letters to a young poet.* Snowball Publishing. (Original work published 1929)

Salzberg, S. (2017). *Real love: The art of mindful connection.* Flatiron Books.

Weill, J.-P. (2016). *A well of being: An extraordinary children's book for adults.* Flatiron Books.

Zemeckis, R. (Director). (1990). *Back to the Future Part III* [Film]. Amblin Entertainment.

Idioms of the Heart

The heart wants what the heart wants
Follow your heart
The heart beats to its own drummer
The heart sees what it wants to see
Home is where the heart is
I heart you
A winged heart
Let's have a heart-to-heart
Eat your heart out
Straight from the heart
A heart of gold
A heart of glass
A heart of stone
A change of heart
A man after your own heart
A broken heart
Be still my beating heart
Hold you in my heart
From the bottom of my heart
From the heart
Good-hearted
Halfhearted
Lighthearted
Kind-hearted
Whole-hearted
Open-hearted
Cold-hearted
Lonely heart
Heatless
Heartbreaker
Faint of heart
Heart and soul
Cross my heart and hope to die
Oh, my aching heart
Heart beating like a drum
Heart jumping like a kangaroo
Bless your heart
In a heartbeat
Queen / King / Jack of hearts
The heart of the matter

Krystal L. Demaine

I have my heart set on it
Dear to my heart
Close to my heart
Don't have the heart
My heart is just not in it
I poured my heart into it
I poured my heart out
She wears her heart on her sleeve
Let's have a heart to heart
Open my heart to you
A heavy heart
Light hearted
Young at heart
Steal my heart
Be still my heart
I know it by heart
Your hearts desire
You make my heart skip a beat
My heart is standing still
You are my heart of hearts
My heart aches for you
Bleeding heart
Kind of heart
Cry your heart out
You melt my heart
Don't break my heart
Put your heart into it
You are the heart of my heart
Absence makes the heart grow fonder
You're in my heart
My heart is yours

Epilogue

Now is the time to tune into the music of the heart. Listen to it, follow it, and create your life experience.

Thank you for reading.

Love, Krystal L. Demaine

Index

A

abortion 105
acorn theory 122
adrenaline 18, 22
afterlife 136
All Souls' Day 117
American Music Therapy Association 72
Aristotle 13
amusia 76-77
ancestral karma 103
ancestral trauma 105, 141
ancestry 121, 131
apple cider vinegar 46-47
Ashkenazi 2, 92, 104
anti-inflammatory 42, 47, 52
anti-Semitism 94
asana 7
asynchopated 13
auditory-motor feedback loop 27
autism (ASD) 27, 49, 66, 72, 79, 91

B

backbend (n.) 7
Beatles, the 69, 84, 137, 142
belonging (belongingness) 82, 89, 102, 124, 127, 130, 131
Berklee College of Music 2, 4, 27, 28, 65, 81 89
bloodline (n.) 91, 92, 105, 120, 121, 127
Brainbow Blueprint 46
broken heart syndrome 17-18
buffalo drum 31

C

cancer 40, 44, 46
chakras 45-46

chameleon effect 52
chant 14, 21, 34, 60, 65, 79, 84, 142, 145
Chinese medicine 8, 45-46, 63, 116
Chinese music 45-46
circadian rhythm 45, 48
coherence 89
consciousness 5, 11, 42, 46, 51, 53, 54, 139-142, 144-145
corpus callosum 1, 76
cortisol 47, 107
COVID-19 5, 17, 28, 42, 71, 128
crystal(s) 42, 64, 90, 115-117
cymatics 40

D

da Vinci, Leonardo 13-14
Das, Krishna 21
Day of the Dead 117
djembe 31, 36, 81
DNA 48, 50, 103-105, 108, 111, 119, 121
drumhead 64
dysregulate 7

E

eardrum 63-64
Earth 42-43, 45, 91, 96, 116, 119, 124, 125
electrocardiogram 18, 20, 25, 30, 50
electromagnetic field 50
emotional understanding 51
Emoto, Masaru 42-43, 63
empathy 27, 40, 49-51, 150, 154-155,
entrainment 48, 80-82

epigenetics 104
expressive arts therapist 6, 127, 128
expressive therapies 3, 6
extrovert 91

F
fetal heartbeat 26-27, 30, 73
fight-or-flight response 19, 79, 107
five-element theory 46
flashback 60, 107
flute 3, 12, 64-69, 83, 138
Frankl, Viktor 128
functional magnetic resonance imaging (not abbreviated) 27

G
gathering drum 4, 31
generations 74, 79, 91, 95, 99-100, 104, 109, 123, 126
grandfather 32, 90, 94, 100
grandmother 94, 104
grandparents 94, 95, 100, 109, 119
Graves, Milford 12-13, 61
grief 3-5, 7-8, 17, 22, 78, 105, 137, 143-145, 150
guitar 73, 84, 99-100, 117, 137-138
gut health 47, 80

H
Hanser, Susanne 27
Hanukkah 132
Harmonium 21
Head Start programs 129
HeartMath 50
heartbeat 4,6,8,11-13, 17,20, 25, 28-35, 42, 61, 73, 81, 139
heartstrings 6, 103, 106
heavy metal 88

Hillman, James 122, 150
Holocaust 104-105, 128
Home 3, 5, 8, 13, 14, 16, 18-20, 22, 25, 31, 34, 36, 40, 41, 60, 71, 72, 90, 95, 99, 108, 117, 124, 126-128, 134, 136, 138, 142, 143, 145
Hungry Ghost Festival 119

I
Inflammation 44, 46-47, 52, 69, 80, 107, 116
inner child 6, 123-125, 150
intergenerational trauma 104
interpersonal neurobiology 101
intimacy 102
intubated 29
iso principle 5, 81

J
Janney, Christopher 12
jazz 2, 3, 11, 13, 65, 95, 100, 138
Jenny, Hans 40
Jewish (jew) 2, 14, 79, 92, 94,-95, 104, 106, 121, 135
joss paper 119
june bug (beetle) 59-60
Jung, Carl 60

K
kaddish 3
Katie, Byron 123
Kaur, Snatam 84, 96, 144-145
kirtan 21, 142, 144
kriah 137
kundalini 53

L
Larrivée 100
Lee, Colin 81-82

life span 36, 33, 65
life support 1, 2
loving 2, 20, 83, 102, 103, 125, 149, 155
lub-dub 11, 25, 35

M

Mantra 21, 55, 109
Martin (guitar) 100, 137
Maslow, Abraham 124 149
meridian 45
mirror neurons 48-49
Montello, Louise 7
Mother 7, 26-31, 34, 50, 52, 73-75, 99, 104, 105, 121, 132, 135, 137, 142, 144, 145
mother ease (parent ease) 75
mudra 151-152
music making 6, 30, 68, 72, 81, 124
music-centered activities 80
musical life review 83, 143
music therapy 2, 4, 6, 25-30, 60, 65, 66, 72, 73, 76, 69, 80, 81, 88, 100, 108, 109, 152-153

N

nadis 45
Native American drum 31
Native American flute 69
nature (n.) 26, 48, 55, 60, 66, 88, 90, 91, 102, 124, 140, 142, 147, 149, 152, 156
near-death experiences (unabbreviated) 139
niggun 79
neonatal ICU 28-29, 72, 75
neuroelectrical 139
neurotransmitter 19, 64
New Year's Day 2, 25
Newborn 3, 28, 29, 32, 51, 73

P

palm (of the hand) 9, 30, 31, 60, 99, 111, 152
parasympathetic nervous system 16, 22, 64, 66, 67, 68
Passamaquoddy tradition (tribe) 31-32
past-life experiences 140
past-life regression therapy 141
pendulum 48, 80
pentatonic scale 45
polarity therapy 116
polyvagal theory 101
Porges, Stephen 101
prana 7, 65, 68, 116
pre- and probiotics 47
PTSD (post-traumatic stress disorder) 18, 105, 107, 128
pulse 6, 11, 14, 25, 26, 28, 30-31, 33-36, 39, 60, 61, 72, 73, 82, 139

Q

qi 14, 45, 116

R

Rabbi 3, 8, 14, 101, 137
regulate 19, 65, 101, 108
relaxation response, the 33, 66
resilience (resiliency, resilient) 71, 89, 124, 128-130, 131, 139, 150
Rilke, Rainer Maria 126, 155
ritual 75, ,106, 131-132, 135

S

saxophone 12
Schreck, Brian 28-30
Schumann resonance 42
shabbat 132, 143
shofar 14

shiva (v.) 135
shy (shyness) 90, 109
sister 1, 2, 3, 25, 26, 52, 84, 90, 94, 125, 137, 138, 142, 145
sleep (sleeping) 27, 40, 46-48, 51-52, 74, 106, 108, 138 ,150
soul 2, 3, 5, 19, 26, 28, 35, 59, 72, 95, 120, 130, 136-137, 152
spirit 3, 4, 5, 14, 22, 26, 30, 31, 32, 71, 72, 130, 131, 136, 136, 142, 143, 145, 147, 149, 155
spiritual 6, 14, 21, 60, 79, 99, 116, 119, 135-136, 142, 143, 145, 155
stress 17-18, 20, 33, 42, 45, 47, 64, 66, 75, 79, 80, 101, 105, 107, 108, 109, 116, 129, 141
Strickland, Stan 11
sympathetic nervous system 16, 17, 22, 67, 108,
synagogue 137
synchronicity 48-50, 60, 80, 81
synesthesia 76-77

T
takotsubo cardiomyopathy 17
Tesla, Nikola 39, 53
timpani 63-64
Tolle, Eckhart 6
Tomb Sweeping Day 119
tradition 32, 74, 79, 92, 119, 131, 135
Transcendental Meditation 33
Tu b' Shvat 92
tuba 61
tubano drum 36

U
unconditional love 21, 124
utero 4, 26, 27, 29, 33, 73,

V
vagus nerve 19, 52, 80, 101

W
water 41-42, 45, 46-47, 52, 65, 71, 145
Weiss, Brian 140-141
Western music 45
Wilkes, Steve 4, 30
whole-body vibration 43
womb 25, 27, 31, 50, 73, 73, 121, 126
Womb Beats 27

Y
Yahrzeit 3, 59, 132, 143
yin and yang 16, 45, 67
yoga 6-7, 8, 21, 25, 33, 48, 52, 53, 64, 65, 68, 81, 88. 108, 116, 117, 142, 149, 151, 153
Yom Kippur 14

Krystal L. Demaine

Author photo by Ezra Demaine.
Reproduced by permission from Ezra Demaine

Krystal L. Demaine, Ph.D., is a board-certified music therapist, registered expressive arts therapist, registered yoga teacher, and Professor of Expressive Therapies in the School of Visual and Performing Arts at Endicott College in Beverly, MA, USA. Her approach to the arts, teaching, therapy and parenting are grounded in science, play, creativity, the power of human connection, and living fully with heart. Her website is www.krystaldemaine.com